**TRAINING,**

MW00856729

REXX with OS/2, TSO & CMS Features Quick Reference Guide

Gabriel F. Gargiulo

sponsored by:

Software superior by design.

**Second Edition: March 2000; First Published 1998.
ISBN 1-892559-03-X**

PUBLISHER

 **TRAINING, INC.**

Your Complete Training Source

600 Airport Professional Office Center
Commerce Drive, Suite 605
Pittsburgh, PA 15108

To order our technical books on-line

www.mvs-training.com

**To discuss your training needs or order technical books, cal
800.356.9093 • Outside US: 412.269.9668
E-mail: sales@mvs-training.com**

om the Editor-in-Chief

abe, who is a very prolific writer of languages, boasts writings that
tend beyond his many well-written technical publications into
reign language publications such as: "Talking to Your Household
elp in Spanish." From my knowledge of Gabe he truly is a "Master
Languages."

an easy–to–use format, Gabe shares with us all there is to know
out the REXX language. For instance, a seasoned REXX user saw
abe's book on my desk and asked if he could borrow the book to
lve a problem. The book provided the answers needed and the
asoned user found the book to be a very valuable reference tool.

you have questions about the REXX language, this is the book for
u. This *REXX with OS/2, TSO, & CMS Features Quick Reference
uide* even covers the compatibility issues across the different
mputer platforms.

edback from readers indicates that Gabe includes items needed
use the REXX language proficiently. Other reader states: "...he
vers everything completely."

here else should you choose to learn a language but from the
aster of Languages." You're referencing the very best. Enjoy!

Olivia R. Carmandi

livia Carmandi
ublisher and Editor-in-Chief
VS TRAINING, INC.
anuary 2000

Thank you to the REXX experts who reviewed the technical content of this book and made suggestions for improvement.

Richard W. Balenger

James Scott Condon

Charles H. Rider

Thank you to the staff at MVS Training, Inc. who assisted in revising, proofreading and final printing of this book.

Krystle G. Bucuren

Shirley J. Calpas

Diane A. Ferner

Sarah N. Weber

Table of Contents

Introduction

REXX is an interpreted language that contains powerful control statements not available in other interpreted languages. Interpreted means when the program runs each statement is translated into codes the computer directly executes.

A major feature of REXX is that the data used by a REXX program can be any type of data. A variable may contain any value as opposed to a language that accepts specific types of data. For instance, in the COBOL programming language when data is defined as numeric, the program accepts only number values. If a value other than a number is used in the numeric variable the program takes an error routine or blows up.

REXX also allows easy character string manipulation and has a powerful set of built-in functions. REXX runs on multiple computer platforms and is easy to learn and use.

This book covers all of the REXX functions, instructions (verbs), and reserved variables including those that exist on OS/2, TSO, and CMS. Any feature that exists on one or more of these platforms is so marked. REXX works very much the same on all platforms, but there are some differences. I show them under the entry COMPATIBILITY ISSUES ACROSS PLATFORMS.

This book does not include add-ons, purchased software, and non-IBM products. Where appropriate I have included OS/2, TSO or CMS commands. These are not part of REXX! I include them because they are commonly used in REXX programs, for example EXECIO, a TSO and CMS command, which can be used only inside of a REXX program.

The index is not like most indexes which list only language features alphabetically. They are no help if you don't know the name of the language feature. This index shows the common English language name for a feature. For example, PERFORM, a COBOL verb, points you to the REXX equivalent CALL.

Some of the OS/2 functions shown will work only if you preregister them with OS/2. I recommend you do what is suggested under RXFUNCADD, below, before you try to use those OS/2 REXX functions.

Before you use any of REXX's built-in functions, please read the entry entitled FUNCTIONS.

For information about REXX directly from the creator of REXX:
   'The REXX Language', Mike Cowlishaw, Publisher Prentice-Hall

will post updates and additional REXX information at http://www.rexxfiles.com

1 REXX Functions
From ABBREV to COMPARE

ABBREV Function

SAY ABBREV(*word, abbrev, length*
Checks whether *abbrev* is a real abbreviation of *word*,
considering *length* characters of *abbrev*. If *length* is omitted,
all of *abbrev* is examined.
Returns a 1 if true, a 0 if false.
Example:

```
SAY ABBREV('OREGON','OR',2)        /* 1 */
SAY ABBREV('OREGON','OR')          /* 1 */
SAY ABBREV('OREGON','ORG',3)       /* 0 */
SAY ABBREV('OREGON','ORG')         /* 0 */
```

Program segment:
```
Say "Who are you? Maria, Beth, or Mario"
Say "please type in your name or abbreviation"
Pull Name /* converts to upper case */
If Abbrev("MARIA",Name) = 1 then say "you must be Maria"
If Abbrev("BETH",Name)  = 1 then say "you must be Beth"
If Abbrev("MARIO",Name) = 1 then say "you must be Mario"
```

ABS Function

SAY ABS(*number*)
Drops the sign of *number*.
Formats the result according to current NUMERIC settings.
Examples:

```
SAY ABS(-123.45)                   /* 123.45 */
SAY ABS(100 - 150)                 /* 50 */
```

ADDRESS Function

SAY ADDRESS()
Returns the current environment that commands are being
sent to.
Returns:

On OS/2:
CMD	{ under OS/2, the normal, standard, default
PMREXX	{ under OS/2 Presentation Manager. OS/2 commands still work

On TSO:
TSO	{ the default, on TSO and ISPF
MVS	{ When running through JCL, executing the REXX interpreter directly. (IRXJCL)
ISPEXEC	{ on TSO, if you have done an ADDRESS ISPEXEC and are executing inside of ISPF

On CMS:
CMS	{ the default on CMS for programs with file type EXEC
COMMAND	{ under CMS if you have done an ADDRESS COMMAND
XEDIT	{ the default on CMS for programs with file type XEDIT (XEDIT macros)

Examples:

```
SAY ADDRESS()          /* CMD or TSO or COMMAND etc */
```

ADDRESS Instruction
Directs REXX to pass commands to a specific environment or command processor.

ADDRESS *environment*
Changes default *environment*.
Subsequent commands will be sent to that environment.

Environments:

Under TSO:

TSO	(the default)
ISPEXEC	(ISPF)
ISREDIT	(ISPF editor)

TSO example:

```
ADDRESS ISPEXEC
"DISPLAY PANEL(PANEL123)"
```

Under CMS:

CMS	(the default for programs whose file type is EXEC)
XEDIT	(the default for programs whose file type is XEDIT: XEDIT macros)
COMMAND	(the CMS command processor, bypasses synonyms, requires uppercase, requires EXEC for EXEC's, CP for CP commands)

CMS example:

```
ADDRESS COMMAND
"SPOOL PRINTER HOLD"
```

Under OS/2:

CMD	the default
PMREXX	(OS/2 Presentation Manager). Note that there is no need to change environments under OS/2, because OS/2 commands can be executed while in the PMREXX environment

ADDRESS *environment* "*command*"
Sends *command* to *environment*. Only the command specified is sent to that environment.

TSO Example:

```
ADDRESS ISPEXEC  "DISPLAY PANEL(PANEL123)"
```

CMS Example:

```
ADDRESS CMS  "PRINT FILE1 DATA A1"
```

ARG Function

SAY ARG()
Asks how many argument strings were passed. (Commas delimit argument strings.) You can pass several to a function/ subroutine, but only one to a main program (executed from the command prompt in an OS/2 Window or Full Screen, XEDIT command line or CMS READY prompt in CMS, ISPF command line, ISPF Option 6, TSO READY prompt in TSO).
Returns a number from 0 up.
Example:

```
CALL SUBR  'SALLY', 'KAREN' 'SUSAN'
EXIT
SUBR:
  SAY ARG()                    /* 2 */
RETURN
```

SAY ARG(*number*)
If *number* is a 1, returns the first argument string. If *number* is a 2, returns the second argument string, and so on.
Example:

```
CALL SUBR 'SALLY', 'KAREN' 'SUSAN'
EXIT
SUBR:
  SAY ARG(2)            /* KAREN SUSAN */
RETURN
```

SAY ARG(*number,* 'EXISTS')

If the argument string numbered *number* exists, it returns a 1; otherwise it returns a 0. EXISTS may be abbreviated 'E.' Only a function or subroutine executed by a REXX CALL may receive more than one argument string. (An argument string is delimited by commas.)

```
Examples:
/* in calling program */
CALL MYEXEC 'SALLY', 'KAREN' 'SUSAN'

/* in called program */
SAY ARG(2,'EXISTS')          /* 1 */

/* in calling program */
CALL MYEXEC 'SALLY', 'KAREN' 'SUSAN'

/* in called program */
SAY ARG(5,'EXISTS')          /* 0 */
```

SAY ARG(*number,* 'OMITTED')

If the argument string numbered *number* was not supplied, it returns a 1; otherwise returns a 0. OMITTED may be abbreviated 'O.'
(An argument string is delimited by commas.)
Examples:

```
/* in calling program */
CALL MYEXEC 'SALLY', 'KAREN' 'SUSAN'

/* in called program */
SAY ARG(2,'OMITTED')        /* 0 */

/* in calling program */
CALL MYEXEC 'SALLY', 'KAREN' 'SUSAN'

/* in called program */
SAY ARG(5,'OMITTED')        /* 1 */
```

ARG Instruction

ARG *variable-1 ... variable-n*
Short form of PARSE UPPER ARG. In a main program it receives
information typed in on the command prompt in an OS/2 Window or
Full Screen, XEDIT command line or CMS READY prompt in CMS,
ISPF command line, ISPF Option 6, TSO READY prompt in TSO.
Commas may not be used here to separate argument strings.
(Because they don't work!) In a function/subroutine it receives
information passed to it on a function invocation or subroutine
call. The information is received in *variable-1* through *variable-n*.
Commas are generally used here to separate argument strings.
Example:

```
ARG FILENAME
/*Executed as MYPROG RESUME.DAT*/
Say FILENAME          /* RESUME.DAT */
```

BEEP Function (OS/2 Only)

CALL BEEP *frequency, duration*
Sounds the speaker at *frequency* for *duration* in milliseconds.
The valid range for *frequency* is from 37 to 32767. The range
for *duration* is from 1 to 60000.
Example:

```
CALL BEEP 1000, 1000   /* listen carefully ... */
```

BITAND Function

SAY BITAND(*string1, string2, pad*)
String1 and *string2* are logically ANDed, with *pad* used to
fill out the shorter string on the right. Each bit in the result
depends on the corresponding bit in *string1* and *string2*.
Each bit in the result is set to a 1 if the corresponding bit in
both strings is a 1; otherwise, the result bit is set to 0.
Example:

```
SAY BITAND('01'X,'0F'X)    /* '01'X */
```

BITOR Function

SAY BITOR(*string1, string2, pad*)

String1 and *string2* are logically ORed, with *pad* used to fill ou
the shorter string on the right. Each bit in the result depends
on the corresponding bit in *string1* and *string2*. Each bit in th
result is set to a 1 if the corresponding bit in either string is a 1
otherwise, the result bit is set to 0.
Example:

```
SAY BITOR('01'X,'0F'X)       /* '0F'X */

SAY BITOR('01'X,'0E'X)       /* '0F'X */
```

BITXOR Function

SAY BITXOR(*string1, string2, pad*)

String1 and *string2* are logically XORed, with *pad* used to fill
out the shorter string on the right. Each bit in the result
depends on the corresponding bit in *string1* and *string2*.
Each bit in the result is set to a 1 if only one of the
corresponding bits (but not both) in either string is a 1,
otherwise the result bit is set to 0.
Example:

```
SAY BITXOR('01'X,'0F'X)       /* '0E'X */

SAY BITXOR('01'X,'0E'X)       /* '0F'X */
```

Boot Drive, what drive did I boot from? OS/2 Only)

```
Boot_Drive  = ,
Filespec("DRIVE",Value("SYSTEM_INI",,"OS2ENVIRONMENT")
```

2X Function

SAY B2X(*string*)
Converts *binary string* to a 'hexadecimal' representation.
Examples:

```
SAY B2X('1111 0000')          /* F0 */
```

ALL Instruction
vokes a subroutine. The subroutine must terminate with a
ETURN instruction. Also turns on or off an error trap that
tercepts an exception condition.

CALL *subroutine* "*string*"
SAY RESULT

String is passed to *subroutine,* which picks it up on its
ARG statement.

Example:

```
CALL MY_SUBR  "ABCD"
```

CALL ON *condition name*

CALL may also be used to initialize an exception condition trap (a subroutine).

If the subroutine is entered, a RETURN at the end will send control back to the instruction after the one that failed.

Condition names:

ERROR
FAILURE
HALT
NOTREADY   /* OS/2 only */

Examples:

```
CALL ON ERROR       /* command to environment (TSO, CMS, OS/
                        not correct */
CALL ON FAILURE     /* command to environment doesn't exist
CALL ON HALT        /* attention interrupt or break  */
                    /* TSO: press PA1 or ATTN
                       CMS: type HI when screen displays
                        More... in lower right
                       OS/2: press CTRL and C or CTRL
                       and Break*/
CALL ON NOTREADY    /* OS/2 only.  Error in input/output
```

Example of a condition trap subroutine that could be used after CALL ON ERROR

ERROR:
   Say "a command to TSO has failed"
   Return

CALL ON *condition name* NAME *new-name*

New-name allows the use of an alternate name for the trap.

Example:

```
CALL ON ERROR NAME MISTAKE
```

Example of a condition trap subroutine that could be used after CALL ON ERROR NAME MISTAKE

```
MISTAKE:
  Say "a command to TSO has failed"
  Return
```

ENTER Function

SAY CENTER(*string, length, pad*)

Centers *string* within a larger string of *length*. *Pad*, if present, is the pad character used instead of spaces.
Examples:

```
SAY CENTER('MIDDLE',14)        /* MIDDLE */

SAY CENTER('MIDDLE',14,'-')  /* -----MIDDLE--- */
```

CHARIN Function (OS/2 and CMS Only)

CALL CHARIN '*file name*'
SAY RESULT

Reads one character from the *file name* specified. Does not recognize end of line, or end of file. To tell if end of file has been reached, check CHARS('*file name*'). If it returns a 0, yo are at the end of the file.

File name may be the name of a data file, or it may be:
   CON:
   KBD:
   COM1: (communications port)
   COM2:
   QUEUE:

Example:

```
/*reads every character in file, one at a time*/
DO WHILE CHARS('C:MYFILE.DAT') > 0
   CALL CHARIN 'C:MYFILE.DAT'
   SAY RESULT
END
```

CALL CHARIN '*file name*', *start char, how many*
SAY RESULT

Reads *how many* characters from the *file name* specified, starting at *start char.* Does not recognize end of line or end c file. To tell if end of file has been reached, check CHARS('*file name*'). If it returns a 0, you are at the end of the file.
Example:

```
/*reads every character in file, one at a time*/
/* starting with the 100'th */
DO WHILE CHARS('C:MYFILE.DAT') > 0
   CALL CHARIN 'C:MYFILE.DAT',100,1
   SAY RESULT
END
```

◢HAROUT Function (OS/2 and CMS Only)

CALL CHAROUT '*file name*', *string*
SAY RESULT

Writes *string* to the *file name* specified. RESULT contains
the number of characters that could not be written, so a 0
indicates a successful write. If the file already exists, it
continues writing after the end of the file.
File name may be the name of a data file, or it may be:
   CON:
   PRN:
   LPT1:
   LPT2:
   COM1: (communications port)
   COM2:
   QUEUE:
   STDERR:

Example:

```
CALL CHAROUT 'C:MYFILE.DAT','This is being written'
SAY RESULT (hopefully a 0)
```

CALL CHAROUT '*file name*', *string, start char*
SAY RESULT

Writes *string* to the *file name* specified. RESULT contains
the number of characters that could not be written, so a 0
indicates a successful write. It starts writing at *start char* and
overwrites whatever may be there. Use a starting character of
1 to start writing at the beginning of the file and overwrite the
entire file.
Example:

```
CALL CHAROUT 'C:MYFILE.DAT','This is being written',100
SAY RESULT (hopefully a 0)
```

CALL CHAROUT 'C:MYFILE.DAT'
This statement, which specifies only the file name, just
closes the file.

CHARS Function (OS/2 and CMS Only)

SAY CHARS('*file name*')

Tells if any characters remain to be read in *file name*. If it returns a 0, there are no more characters remaining in the file meaning that it is at the end of file.
Example:

```
/*reads every character in file, one at a time*/
DO WHILE CHARS('C:MYFILE.DAT') > 0
    CALL CHARIN 'C:MYFILE.DAT'
    SAY RESULT
END
```

Comment.
A REXX comment begins with /* and ends with */. It may start an end on different lines.

Example:

```
/* This is a comment */
Say "HELLO" /* this is a comment */
/* this is a comment
    too
*/
```

Comment, initial
To ensure compatibility on all platforms, it must begin in column of the first line of the program, and the word REXX must be in it somewhere.
Example:

```
/* REXX anything */
or
/* REXX anything
    anything else
*/
```

CMSFLAG Function (CMS Only)

SAY CMSFLAG(*setting*)

Returns information about the internal CMS *setting*.
If the setting is on, it returns a 1; otherwise, a 0.
Settings:

ABBREV   if abbreviations of commands allowed ---> 1
                if abbreviations not allowed ---> 0

AUTOREAD   if console read is to be done
                after command execution ---> 1
                otherwise ---> 0

CMSTYPE   if commands are to display their output
                at the terminal ---> 1
                otherwise ---> 0

DOS   if DOS environment is on ---> 1
                otherwise ---> 0

EXECTRAC   if EXECTRAC is on ---> 1
                otherwise ---> 0

IMPCP   if "CP" is implied before CP commands
                ---> 1
                otherwise ---> 0

IMPEX   if "EXEC" is implied before EXECS
                ---> 1
                otherwise ---> 0

PROTECT   if CMS nucleus is storage protected ---> 1
                otherwise ---> 0

RELPAGE   if pages are to be released after command execution ---> 1
                otherwise ---> 0

SUBSET   if you are in CMS subset ---> 1
                otherwise ---> 0

Examples:

```
SET IMPEX ON
SAY CMSFLAG("IMPEX")                    /* 1 */
```

COMPARE Function

SAY COMPARE(*string1, string2, pad*)

Compares *string1* to *string2*. *Pad*, if present, is the pad character used to fill out the shorter string. If *pad* is not present, spaces are used. If both strings are equal, it returns a 0; otherwise, it returns the character position of inequality. Examples:

```
SAY COMPARE('APPLES','APPLES')          /* 0 */

SAY COMPARE('APPLES','APPLESAUCE')      /* 7 */
```

Compatibility Issues across different platforms

2

Initial comment:

CMS	required in first line
TSO	required in first line with word REXX if library/PDS containing program has been allocated to DDNAME SYSPROC. not required if library/PDS containing program has been allocated to DDNAME SYSEXEC
OS/2	required in first line, in first character position

Compatible solution on all platforms:
use comment containing REXX, in first line, first character position

Concatenation || or logical OR symbol |
Many different keyboards and emulations exist.
Mainframe emulations often require you to press the
[ ] or I key
File Transfer utilities may not translate correctly.

CMS and TSO	require unbroken vertical bar, hex 4F
OS/2	require broken vertical bar, hex 7C (the "pipe" symbol)

Compatible solutions on all platforms:
You may concatenate data strings as follows:
Variable and a literal:　　　　Name" is my name"
(variable and literal juxtaposed)
Variable and a variable:　　　　Name""Last_name
(null string between)

Literal and a function   "Name is
          "Length(Name)" characters long"
The logical OR can not be easily avoided.
    A SELECT may be used, at the expense of simplicit♦
    Example:
          Instead of:
                    If A = 1 I A = 2 then /* instruction */
                    ELSE /* instruction */
          You might use:
                    SELECT
                        WHEN A = 1 then /* instruction*
                        WHEN A = 2 then /* instruction ♦
                    OTHERWISE /* instruction */
                              END
If you use these symbols, check for validity after uploading/
downloading and ASCII/EBCDIC conversion, by executing
every line of code that contains them

Logical NOT symbol ¬
    many different keyboards and emulations exist.
    File Transfer utilities may not translate correctly.

CMS and TSO   accept ¬, hex 5F
                               do not accept ^,
OS/2   does not accept ¬, hex 5F
                               accepts ^

Compatible solutions on all platforms:
                    use the backslash \ for logical NOT
                    use <> for NOT EQUAL
                    avoid the NOT altogether, by making the logic
                    positive, and using the ELSE for the negative
                    outcome

Sorting sequence:
    CMS and TSO   numbers before letters
                               lower case before upper case
    OS/2   letters before numbers
                               upper case before lower case

Compatible solution on all platforms:
>   None
Length of data strings placed in the Data Queue
>   CMS   255 bytes
>   TSO   > 255 bytes
>   OS/2   > 255 bytes

Compatible solution on all platforms:
>   limit items placed in the queue to 255 bytes

The Data Queue/Stack;
>   TSO and CMS   items left in the Stack are passed to the operating system which tries to execute them as commands
>   OS/2   items left in the default "SESSION" Data Queue survive the program but are deleted when the window (session) is closed.
>   items left in a named, private Data Queue survive the program, the window, and a boot. To delete them, explicitily delete the Queue.

Compatible solutions on all platforms:
>   Clean out the Queue/Stack at the end of the program and in all condition traps ending with an EXIT
>   DO QUEUED(); PULL; END

>   If In doubt as to whether there might be anything left over in the Queue, use this code to clean out the Queue
>   DO QUEUED(); PULL; END

Quotes/apostrophes around environment commands:
>   Both types work on all systems.
>   Of course, you must end with the same type that you started with.
>   "ERASE ABC DATA A" or 'ERASE ABC DATA A'
>   "LISTALC STATUS" or 'LISTALC STATUS'

CMS either type just fine
      "SPOOL READER HOLD"
      'SPOOL READER HOLD'

TSO " may be preferred, because some TSO
    commands use ' so " will avoid conflict.
    "SEND 'HELLO THERE' USER(TSOU01)"
    "DELETE 'TSOU02.TEMP.DATA' "

OS/2 ' may be preferred, because some OS/2
    commands use " so ' will avoid conflict.
    'START "THIS IS THE TITLE" /F /C
    MYPROG1.CMD '

Compatible solution on all platforms:
    None. Use whichever you feel is more appro-
    priate. Since this applies only to environment
    commands, you may continue to use whicheve
    you prefer for literals.

Return codes:
 These are three different operating systems They don't
 give the same return codes for similar situations!

CMS unknown CMS or CP command gives -3 return
    code

TSO unknown TSO command gives -3 return code
    if addressing ISPEXEC or ISREDIT you may get
    an ISPF dialog error

OS/2 unknown OS/2 command gives 1041 return
    code

Compatible solution on all platforms:
    Check for non-zero return codes.
    Test programs carefully.

Continuing literals over several lines:

CMS	these work
	Say "Hello it is a very nice
	day, do you agree?"
	Say "Hello it is a very nice " ,
	"day, do you agree?" /* you may use
	concatenation symbol before comma
	on first line to delete excess spaces*/
TSO	these work
	Say "Hello it is a very nice
	day, do you agree?"
	Say "Hello it is a very nice " ,
	"day, do you agree?" /* you may use
	concatenation symbol before comma on first
	line to delete excess spaces*/
OS/2	this works
	Say "Hello it is a very nice " ,
	"day, do you agree?" /* you may use
	concatenation symbol before comma on first
	line to delete excess spaces*/

Compatible solution:

```
        Say "Hello it is a very nice " ,
        "day, do you agree?" /* you may use
        concatenation symbol before comma on first
        line to delete excess spaces*/
```

Instructions (REXX verbs)
ENDLOCAL and SETLOCAL exist on OS/2 only

Trace C does nothing when executing in an OS/2 window
(it's the default) it does, however work when executing in
Presentation manager
Trace ! does not inhibit environment command execution
on OS/2 (syntax error)

SIGNAL ON NOTREADY exists on OS/2 only
Parse [Upper] Linein exists on OS/2 only.

These functions exist only on OS/2
>Beep
>Endlocal
>Rxfuncadd
>Rxqueue
>Setlocal
>Syscls
>Syscreateobject
>Syscurpos
>Syscurstate
>Sysderegisterobjectclass
>Sysdestroyobject
>Sysdriveinfo
>Sysdrivemap
>Sysdropfuncs
>Sysfiledelete
>Sysfilesearch
>Sysfiletree
>Sysgetea
>Sysgetkey
>Sysgetmessage
>Sysmkdir
>Sysos2ver
>Sysputea
>Sysqueryclasslist
>Sysregisterobjectclass
>Sysrmdir
>Syssearchpath
>Sysseticon
>Syssleep
>Systempfilename
>Systextscreenread
>Systextscreensize
>Syswaitnamedpipe

These functions do not exist on OS/2
>FIND
>EXTERNALS
>STORAGE
>USERID

These functions exist only on TSO
>LISTDSI
>MSG
>OUTTRAP
>SYSDSN
>SYSVAR

These functions exist only on CMS
>CMSFLAG
>DIAGRC

3 Compound Variables

Compound Variables

REXX compound variables are like subscripted variables in programming languages like COBOL and BASIC. The major difference is that the "subscript" may actually contain a character string.
Examples:

```
Day.1 = "Mon"
Variable = 1
Say Day.Variable      /* gives Mon */

Student = "Joe"
Grade.Student = 98.6
Say Grade.Student     /* gives 98.6 */
```

Concatenating 4

Concatenating data strings.

The concatenation operator (ll) may be used to join two items, data strings, variables, literals or functions.
All spaces between the two items will be deleted.
Please note that the symbol (ll) may introduce compatibility problems across platforms; see the entry on compatibility.

Example:

```
Say "the answer is " || 4 * 5 || "%"
```

Concatenating to **SYSPROC/SYSEXEC** (TSO Only)

I'll give you two ways. First, a TSO command that you can type in. Then a REXX program.
You may manually type in the following from TSO/ISPF Option 6, TSO Commands. It must be re-entered everytime you get into ISPF and must be entered on each half of an ISPF split screen. Prefix it with TSO space if you enter it on an ISPF screen other than Option 6.

```
ALTLIB ACTIVATE APPLICATION(EXEC) DA(your-rexx-library)
```

Or you may use the program CATNATE that is available on the Internet.
Download it from here:
http://members.aol.com/rexxauthor/download/catnate.txt

5 REXX Functions
From CONDITION to FORMAT

CONDITION Function

SAY CONDITION(*type*)
When used in a condition trap (ERROR, FAILURE, NOVALUE, HALT, SYNTAX), it gives information about the condition that occurred.

Types:

C — gives name of the condition that occurred: (ERROR, FAILURE, NOVALUE, HALT, SYNTAX)

D — when possible, gives the string that actually caused the error.

I — gives the instruction that sent to the trap: SIGNAL or CALL.

S — gives the current status of the condition that was trapped: ON, OFF, or DELAY (currently trapped, further trapping disabled to avoid recursive entry to the trap).

Examples:

```
SIGNAL ON ERROR
'LISTCAT DOG'                /* on TSO */
'PRINT NOTTHERE JUNK A1 '    /* on CMS */
'DIR X.X.X' /* on OS/2 */
EXIT
ERROR:
SAY CONDITION('C')           /* ERROR */
SAY CONDITION('D')           /* LISTCAT DOG or 'PRINT NOTTHERE JUNK A1 '
                                or 'DIR X.X.X' */
EXIT
```

CONWAIT CMS Command (CMS Only)
"CONWAIT"

This CMS command waits until all output directed to the terminal has been displayed. Often used with DESBUF to assure that no terminal display is lost while clearing the terminal output buffer.
Example:

```
PUSH "CART"
"CONWAIT"
"DESBUF" /* CART is lost */
```

COPIES Function

SAY COPIES(*string, how many*)
Returns *how many* copies of *string*, side by side.
Examples:

```
SAY COPIES('DO',2)    /* DODO */

SAY COPIES('DO',0)    /*  (zero characters, or the
                          null string)  */
```

C2D Function

SAY C2D(*string*)
Converts *string* to a binary representation, then to a decimal value.

OS/2 Examples:

```
SAY C2D('B')              /* 66 */

SAY C2D('b')              /* 98 */

SAY C2D('10'X)            /* 16 */
```

TSO and CMS Examples:

```
SAY C2D('B')              /* 194 */

SAY C2D('b')              /* 130 */

SAY C2D('82'X)            /* 130 */
```

C2X Function

SAY C2X(*string*)
Converts *string* to a 'hexadecimal' representation.

OS/2 Example:

```
SAY C2X('A123')           /* 41313233 */
```

TSO and CMS Example:

```
SAY C2X('A123')           /* C1F1F2F3 */
```

DATATYPE Function

SAY DATATYPE(*string*)
Returns NUM if *string* is a valid number; otherwise, CHAR.
Examples:

```
SAY DATATYPE(1234)        /* NUM */
SAY DATATYPE(X234)        /* CHAR */
```

SAY DATATYPE(*string, type*)
Returns 1 if *string* corresponds to *type*; otherwise, 0.
Note: You may need to strip extraneous spaces for this to work:
Example:

```
SAY "Please type in your name"
PULL Name
SAY DATATYPE(SPACE(Name,0),'U')
```

Types:

A   alphanumeric A-Z, a-z, 0-9
B   binary digits 1 and 0
C   mixed normal and double byte character set
D   double byte character set
L   lower case letters
M   mixed case
N   valid number
S   symbol: valid REXX symbol
U   upper case letters
W   whole number
X   hexadecimal number   0-9 or A-F

Examples:

```
SAY DATATYPE('A234','N')        /* 0 */
SAY DATATYPE('A234','A')        /* 1 */
SAY DATATYPE('ABCDEF','U')      /* 1 */
SAY DATATYPE('aBCDEF','U')      /* 0 */
```

DATE Function

SAY DATE()
Returns current date in format 25 Dec 2000.
Example:

```
SAY DATE()        /* 25 Dec 2000 */
```

SAY DATE(*type*)
Returns date corresponding to *type*.

Types:

B   basedate: number of complete days since January 1, year 1. Example: 727024.

C   century: number of days since January 1, 1900. Example: 33430.

D   days: number of days so far this year. Example: 193.

E   European date: format dd/mm/yy

J   Julian date: format yyddd

M   Name of current month

N   Normal the default format 25 Dec 1997

O   Ordered: date suitable for sorting: yy/mm/dd

S   Sorting: date suitable for sorting: yyyymmdd

U   USA format: mm/dd/yy

W   Name of current weekday

Examples:

```
SAY DATE('W')              /* Friday */
SAY DATE('J')              /* 20359 */
SAY DATE('S')              /* 20001225 */
```

DELSTACK TSO Command (TSO Only)

"DELSTACK"
Deletes a stack created by NEWSTACK and all that is in the stack.
If there are no stacks created by NEWSTACK it clears out the default normal stack.
Example:

```
"DELSTACK"
```

DELSTR Function

SAY DELSTR(*string, start char, length*)
Deletes characters from *string* beginning at *start char*,
for a length of *length.*
Examples:

```
SAY DELSTR('ABCDEF',2,3)              /* AEF */

/* a way to remove a string from within another string */
BIGSTR = 'ISSUES'
DELET  = 'SUE'
NEWSTR =,
DELSTR(BIGSTR,POS(DELET,BIGSTR),LENGTH(DELET))
SAY NEWSTR /* ISS */
```

DELWORD Function

SAY DELWORD(*string, start word, how many words*)
Deletes *how many words* words from *string*, beginning with
start word.
Example:

```
SAY DELWORD('Mary had a little lamb',2,3) /* Mary lamb */
```

DESBUF CMS Command (CMS Only)

"DESBUF"
This CMS command clears the stack and the terminal input
and output buffers.
Often used with CONWAIT, which assures that no terminal
display is lost while clearing the buffer.
Examples:

```
PUSH "CART"
"CONWAIT"
"DESBUF" /* CART is lost */
```

DIAGRC Function (CMS Only)

SAY DIAGRC(*code, "command to CP"*)

Passes *code* to CP, and the *command to CP.* Reply from CP is
the result of the function. A return code from CP is included in
the first 11 bytes of the reply. Use of this function should be lim
ited to those already familiar with the workings of CP commands
Example:

```
SAY DIAGRC(8,"QUERY READER")    /* 0   NO RDR FILES *
```

DIGITS Function

SAY DIGITS()

Returns the current setting of NUMERIC DIGITS.
Example:

```
NUMERIC DIGITS 7
SAY DIGITS()                    /* 7 */
```

DIRECTORY Function (OS/2 Only)

CALL DIRECTORY 'directory'
SAY RESULT

Captures the current directory in the special variable RESULT
and then changes the current directory to *directory.*
Example:

```
CALL DIRECTORY 'C:\REXXPRGS'
SAY RESULT 'WAS THE DIRECTORY BEFORE'
```

CALL DIRECTORY ""
SAY RESULT

Captures the current directory in the special variable RESULT.
Example:

```
CALL DIRECTORY ""
SAY RESULT 'IS THE CURRENT DIRECTORY'
```

D2C Function

SAY D2C(*number*)
Converts a decimal *number* to an ASCII or EBCDIC value.
The inverse of C2D. Like the ASC function in BASIC.

OS/2 Examples: (ASCII)

```
SAY D2C(66)                    /* B */

SAY D2C(98)                    /* b */
```

TSO and CMS Examples: (EBCDIC)

```
SAY D2C(194)                   /* B */

SAY D2C(130)                   /* b */
```

D2X Function

SAY D2X(*number*)
Converts a decimal *number* to a hexadecimal value.
The inverse of X2D.
Examples:

```
SAY D2X(130)          /* 82 */

SAY D2X(15)           /* F */
```

DO Instruction

Begins a group of instructions that are performed repeatedly, controlled by a variable or a REXX language element.
Examples:

```
DO I = 1 to 10 /* incrementing a variable */
  SAY I
END

/* subtracts 1 from the variable each time through the loop*/
DO I = 10 TO 1 BY -1
  SAY "COUNTDOWN " I
END


/* loops without limit; end loop with LEAVE instruction */
DO FOREVER
  IF TIME() > "16:00:00" THEN LEAVE
END
DO UNTIL TIME > "16:00:00" /* loops until a condition is true *
  SAY "WORK"
END
DO WHILE TIME < "16:00:00" /* as long as a condition is true *
  SAY "WORK"
END

DO 10 /* loops a fixed number of times */
    SAY "HELLO"
END
```

DROP Instruction

DROP *variable*
Undefines *variable*. Causes REXX to take the string (which previously was a variable) as a literal, equal to its name, but uppercased.
Example:

```
GREETING = "HELLO"
SAY GREETING          /* HELLO */
DROP GREETING
SAY GREETING          /* GREETING */
```

DROPBUF TSO and CMS Command (TSO and CMS Only)

"DROPBUF"
Deletes a buffer created by MAKEBUF. Please see MAKEBUF for an example of DROPBUF.

D2X Function

SAY D2X(*number*)
Converts a decimal *number* to a hexadecimal value. The inverse of X2D.
Examples:

```
SAY D2X(130)           /* 82 */

SAY D2X(15)            /* F */
```

END Instruction
Terminates a group of instructions controlled by a DO. Terminates a SELECT structure. See DO.

END *variable*
Terminates a group of instructions controlled by a DO that increments *variable*. *Variable* is optional, but is used to make it easier to check for matching DO's and END's.
Example:

```
DO I = 1 TO 10
  SAY I
END I
```

ENDLOCAL Function (OS/2 Only)

CALL ENDLOCAL
SAY RESULT

Restores the drive directory and environment variables that were in effect before the last SETLOCAL function was done. A 1 is returned in RESULT if the command was successful; a 0 is returned if it was not successful. If you do a SETLOCAL and end the program without doing an ENDLOCAL, it is done for you.
Example:

```
CALL ENDLOCAL
SAY RESULT
```

ENDLOCAL Instruction (OS/2 Only)

Restores the current drive and directory that were saved by a SETLOCAL instruction. If you do a SETLOCAL and end the program without doing an ENDLOCAL, it is done for you.
Example:

```
ENDLOCAL
```

ERRORTEXT Function

SAY ERRORTEXT(*number*) Returns the REXX syntax error message corresponding to *number*.
Generally used in a SYNTAX trap.
Example:

```
SAY ERRORTEXT(16)              /* LABEL NOT FOUND */
```

XECIO TSO and CMS Command (TSO and CMS Only)

This TSO/CMS command interacts with REXX to allow you to
read and write files in a REXX EXEC.
On TSO, a TSO command "ALLOCATE" must connect a
dataset to a DDNAME before you can execute "EXECIO."

EXECIO return codes on TSO and CMS

0	successful
1	truncation on DISKW
2	end of file on DISKR or DISKRU
4	empty concatenated dataset on DISKR or DISKRU (can apply only to TSO)
20	fatal error - no data transferred

CMS Examples:

```
CMS: (filename, filetype, filemode stand for the actual file
being read or written).

"EXECIO * CARD "/*reads from reader, puts records into sta */

"EXECIO * CARD (STEM RECD.)" /* reads from the reader, puts
records into array RECD.1 through RECD.n,
where n is the number of records read.
EXECIO sets RECD.0 to the number of records read.

"EXECIO " RECD.0 "PRINT (STEM RECD.)" /* writes the contents of
array RECD.1 through RECD.n to the printer */

"EXECIO " RECD.0 "PUNCH (STEM RECD.)" /* writes the contents of
array RECD.1 through RECD.n to the punch */

"EXECIO " QUEUED() "PRINT " /*writes contents of stack to the
printer */

"EXECIO " QUEUED() "PUNCH " /* writes the contents of the stack
to the punch */

"EXECIO * DISKR filename filetype filemode " /* reads a file,
puts all records into stack */
```

"EXECIO * DISKR *filename filetype filemode* (STEM RECD.)" /* read a file, puts all records into array RECD.1 through RECD.n *

"EXECIO " QUEUED() " DISKW *filename filetype filemode* " /* write the contents of the stack to a file */

"EXECIO " RECD.0 " DISKW *filename filetype filemode* (STEM RECD.) /* writes the contents of the array RECD.1 through RECD.n to a file */

"EXECIO 1 DISKRU *filename filetype filemode* " /* reads a record into stack, holds record for rewrite */

"EXECIO 1 DISKRU *filename filetype filemode* (VAR RECORD)" /* reads a record into variable RECORD, holds record for rewrite*

"EXECIO 1 CP (STRING QUERY READER ALL)" /* passes the command QUERY READER ALL to CP and receives one line of the reply from CP in the stack */

"FINIS *filename filetype filemode*" /* closes a file */

TSO Examples:

TSO: (*ddname* stands for the DDNAME that is allocated to the file that is being read or written).

"EXECIO * DISKR *ddname* (FINIS)" /* reads a file, puts all records into the stack, closes the file */

"EXECIO * DISKR *ddname* (STEM RECD. FINIS)" /* reads a file, puts all records into array RECD.1 through RECD.n, closes the file*/

"EXECIO " QUEUED() " DISKW *ddname* (FINIS) " /* writes the contents of the stack to a file, closes the file */

"EXECIO " RECD.0 " DISKW *ddname* (STEM RECD. FINIS)" /* writes the contents of the array RECD.1 through RECD.n to a file*/

"EXECIO 1 DISKRU *ddname* " /* reads a record into stack, holds record for rewrite */

:XECUTIL TSO Command (TSO Only)

This TSO command is used to influence the execution of
REXX EXEC's.
It may be executed inside of an PROGRAM or as a TSO
command outside of the EXEC.

"EXECUTIL *command*"
Executes *command,* which affects the execution of a REXX
EXEC. Normally found inside of an EXEC, but may be exe-
cuted as a TSO command during interactive debug.
Examples:

```
"EXECUTIL TS" turns on interactive debug with an automatic
TRACE RESULTS.

"EXECUTIL TE" turns off interactive debug.

"EXECUTIL HT" stops display to the terminal from a SAY, eveN
another PROGRAM that you may execute.

"EXECUTIL RT" resumes display to the terminal.

"EXECUTIL HI" stops execution of the program.
```

"EXECUTIL SEARCHDD(YES)"
Generally executed before the first REXX PROGRAM of the
session, it causes TSO to search for REXX EXEC's in the
dataset allocated to the DDNAME SYSEXEC, (as contrasted
with the default SYSPROC). Normally not found inside of a
REXX program.

EXIT Instruction

Ends the REXX program and returns control to the caller, whatever the caller may be.

May pass back a return code (numeric only) to the caller.

If caller is TSO, the return code may be examined by the WHEN TSO command.

If the caller is CMS, the return code is displayed at the terminal

If the caller is a REXX program, the return code may by exam ined by the RC special variable.

If the caller is a CLIST, the return code may be examined by the special variables &MAXCC and &LASTCC.

Under OS/2, if the caller is a batch file, the return code may be examined by the IF ERRORLEVEL command.

Examples:

```
EXIT
EXIT 8
```

EXPOSE keyword on the PROCEDURE Instruction

EXPOSE *variable-1 ... variable-n*

Used with the PROCEDURE instruction on an internal function subroutine to allow *variable-1* through *variable-n* to be shared with the main part of the program.

Makes those variables global. Generally found right after the internal function/subroutine's label.

Example:

```
SUBR: PROCEDURE EXPOSE VAR1 /* VAR1 is shared with the main part
of the program; all others are protected. */
```

ILESPEC Function

halyzes a file specification and tells whichever of the following is
quested: Drive, Path, Name of the file.
  Examples:

```
SAY FILESPEC('DRIVE','C:\REXXPRGS\TEST.DAT')   /* C: */
SAY FILESPEC('PATH','C:\REXXPRGS\TEST.DAT')    /* \REXXPRGS\*/
SAY FILESPEC('NAME','C:\REXXPRGS\TEST.DAT')    /* TEST.DAT */
```

XTERNALS Function (TSO and CMS Only)

SAY EXTERNALS()
In CMS/REXX, returns the number of elements in the terminal
input buffer (how many lines were typed ahead).
In TSO/REXX, always returns a 0 because you cannot
type ahead.
Examples:

```
SAY EXTERNALS()    /* 0   (under TSO)   */

SAY EXTERNALS()    /* 0   (under CMS, possibly) */
```

IND Function (TSO and CMS Only)

SAY FIND(*string, phrase*)
Returns the word number of the first word of *phrase* in *string*.
Example:

```
SAY FIND('MARY HAD A LITTLE LAMB','A LITTLE LAMB')  /* 3 */
```

FORM Function

SAY FORM()
Returns the current setting of NUMERIC FORM.
Example:

```
SAY FORM()/* SCIENTIFIC  (the default) or ENGINEERING *
```

FORMAT Function

SAY FORMAT(*number, before decimal, after decimal*)
Formats a *number*. *Before decimal* is the number of
characters before the decimal point, padded with blanks.
After decimal is the number of characters after the decimal
point, zero filled.
Example:

```
SAY FORMAT(123.45,5,3)/* 123.450 */
```

Functions 6

FUNCTIONS

All of REXX's built in functions may be used in two ways:

1. Substitution: REXX replaces the function name with the result or answer from the function, for example:

```
SAY LENGTH('ABCDEF') /*becomes SAY 6, which then
 displays a "6" at the terminal or monitor*/

SAVE_LENGTH = LENGTH(NAME)          /* assignment */

SAY 'NAME CONTAINS ',
     LENGTH(NAME) ' LETTERS'       /* substitution */

SAY "DOUBLING YOUR NAME'S LENGTH GIVES",
     LENGTH(NAME) * 2 'LETTERS'/* arith. expression */
```

Notes:
- *There must not be a space between the name of the function and the parenthesis.*
- *The result of the function is not available in the variable RESULT.*
- *Please separate parameters with commas, not spaces. Example: LEFT('ABCD',2)*

2. Using CALL and the reserved variable RESULT to obtain the result of the function's processing, for example:

```
CALL LENGTH 'ABCDEF'
SAY RESULT      /* result contains 6, which is displayed

CALL LENGTH 'ABCDEF'
SAVE_LENGTH = RESULT           /* assignment */


CALL LENGTH NAME
SAY 'NAME CONTAINS ',
     RESULT ' LETTERS'      /* substitution*/

CALL LENGTH NAME
SAY"DOUBLING YOUR NAME'S LENGTH GIVES",
     RESULT * 2 ' LETTERS ' /* arithmetic expression *
```

Notes:
- *You must do a CALL if you wish to receive the result of the function in the variable RESULT.*
- *Please separate parameters with commas, not spaces. Example: CALL LEFT 'ABCD',2.*
- *Parentheses are not used.*

Functions classified by type

Character string manipulation

Retrieve information, don't change anything
Abbreviation, is a string an abbrev?	ABBREV
Character or numeric?	DATATYPE
Character string an abbrev. of another?	ABBREV
Compare two strings	COMPARE
Count words in a string	WORDS
Length of a string	LENGTH
Locate word in a string	WORD, WORDINDEX
Numeric or character?	DATATYPE
Parameters, prompt line	ARG
Position of one string in another	INDEX, POS, LASTPOS, WORDPOS

Prompt line parameters	ARG
String length	LENGTH
String, position of one in another	INDEX, POS, LASTPOS, WORDPOS
Strings, compare two	COMPARE
Symbol, is it a legal REXX symbol?	SYMBOL
Variable, is it one?	SYMBOL
Word in a string, locate one	WORD, WORDINDEX
Words in a string, count them	WORDS

Retrieve changed information

Align to the right	JUSTIFY
Center a string within another	CENTER
Characters, convert to other characters	TRANSLATE
Characters, delete	DELSTR
Delete characters from a string	DELSTR
Delete words from a sentence	DELWORD
Insert a string into another	INSERT
Reproduce a string	COPIES
Right alignment	JUSTIFY
Spaces, delete from a string	STRIP
Spaces, insert into or delete from a string	SPACE
String centering within another	CENTER
String copy	COPIES
String with characters in reverse order	REVERSE
String, insert	INSERT
String, leftmost characters	LEFT
String, part of	SUBSTR
String, rightmost characters	RIGHT
Upper case, convert	TRANSLATE
Variable, examine its contents	VALUE
Word in a string, give specified word	SUBWORD
Words, delete	DELWORD

Convert datatype
    Binary to hexadecimal   B2X
    Character to decimal   C2D
    Character to hexadecimal   C2X
    Decimal to character   D2C
    Decimal to hexadecimal   D2X
    Hexadecimal to binary   X2B
    Hexadecimal to character   X2C
    Hexadecimal to decimal   X2D

Numeric
    Format a number   FORMAT
    Highest number of a series   MAX
    Lowest number of a series   MIN
    Pseudo-random number   RANDOM
    Random number   RANDOM
    Sign, determine   SIGN
    Sign, drop   ABS
    Truncate decimal positions   TRUNC

Environment, interact with
    Clear the screen   SYSCLS
    Conditions   CONDITION
    Cursor position   SYSCURPOS
    Cursor visibility   SYSCURSTATE
    Data Queue, lines in   QUEUED
    Date   DATE
    Directory, tell current one
    and / or change it   DIRECTORY
    Drive information   SYSDRIVEINFO,
                                   SYSDRIVEMAP

    Environment, what is it   ADDRESS

Environment: return information about the operating system or REXX options

Command, capture display on TSO	OUTTRAP
Error message from REXX	ERRORTEXT
Information about OS/2 profile variables	SYSINI
Line of program	SOURCELINE
Message box, display	RXMESSAGEBOX
Message, error	ERRORTEXT
Messages from TSO commands, control	MSG
Messages, retrieve	SYSGETMESSAGE
Numeric digits setting	DIGITS
Numeric form setting	FORM
Numeric fuzz setting	FUZZ
Pipe, wait for	SYSWAITNAMEDPIPE
Program text	SOURCELINE
Read characters off the screen	SYSTEXTSCREENREAD
Restore drive and directory information	ENDLOCAL
Save drive and directory information	SETLOCAL
Size of screen, return	SYSTEXTSCREENSIZE
Suspend execution	SYSSLEEP
Text of program	SOURCELINE
Time	TIME
Tone, sound	BEEP
TSO information	SYSVAR
Version of OS/2	SYSOS2VER

Files, interacting with

Characters remaining to be read	CHARS
Directories, search through	SYSFILETREE
Directory, create	SYSMKDIR
Directory, delete	SYSRMDIR
Extended attributes, change	SYSPUTEA
Extended attributes, retrieve	SYSGETEA
File access, general function	STREAM
File search in one	SYSFILESEARCH
File specification, analyze	FILESPEC
File, delete	SYSFILEDELETE
File, give attributes on TSO	LISTDSI, SYSDSN
File, return unique temporary file name	SYSTEMPFILENAME
File, search through path to find	SYSSEARCHPATH
Read a character	CHARIN
Read a record	LINEIN
Records remaining to be read	LINES
Write a character	CHAROUT
Write a record	LINEOUT

Functions, interacting with

Drop functions	RXFUNCDROP, SYSDROPFUNCS
Query	RXFUNCQUERY
Register certain OS/2 specific functions	RXFUNCADD

Objects, interacting with

Classes, register	SYSREGISTEROBJECTCLASS
Classes, show names of	SYSQUERYCLASSLIST
Create	SYSCREATEOBJECT
Destroy	SYSDESTROYOBJECT
Object class	SYSDEREGISTEROBJECTCLAS

REXX Functions   **7**
From FUZZ to LISTDSI

FUZZ Function

SAY FUZZ()
Returns the current setting of NUMERIC FUZZ.
Examples:

```
SAY FUZZ()        /* 0 */
NUMERIC FUZZ 5
SAY FUZZ()        /* 5 */
```

HI TSO and CMS Command (TSO and CMS Only)
Stops execution of the program.

> • On TSO, it may be executed after an attention interrupt
> obtained by pressing the PA1 key or the ATTN key.

> • On CMS, it may be executed as a CMS immediate command
> when the screen is displaying MORE ... in the lower right.

HT TSO and CMS Command (TSO and CMS Only)
Stops display to the terminal.

> • On TSO, it may be executed after an attention interrupt
> obtained by pressing the PA1 key or the ATTN key.

> • On CMS, it may be executed as a CMS immediate command
> when the screen is displaying MORE ... in the lower right.

IF Instruction

> **IF** *expression*
> **THEN** *instruction*
> **ELSE** *instruction*

Controls conditional execution of one or more instructions.
Checks to see if *expression* is true.
If it is, then the *instruction* after the THEN is executed.
If it is false, then the *instruction* after the ELSE is executed.
IF allows only one instruction after the THEN or the ELSE,
    but a DO . . . END sequence will allow use of more
    than one instruction.

Expression may use one of these comparison operators:

=   **Equal**. If numeric, when compared algebraically.
        (1.0 is equal to 001.000.) If not numeric, when padded
        with leading or trailing spaces. ("Sue" is equal to "
        Sue "). Case is significant: "SUE" is not equal to "sue.

<>   **Not equal**, the negation of "=." Algebraic comparison
        and padding are performed.

><   **Not equal**, the negation of "=." Algebraic comparison
        and padding are performed.

\=   **Not equal**, the negation of "=." Algebraic comparison
        and padding are performed.

¬=   **Not equal**, the negation of "=." (The symbol "¬" may
        not be found on all keyboards.) Algebraic comparison
        and padding are performed.

^=   **Not equal**, the negation of "=." (The symbol "^" may
        not be found on all keyboards.) Algebraic comparison
        and padding are performed.

>   **Greater than**. Algebraic comparison and padding
        are performed.

< **Less than**. Algebraic comparison and padding are performed.

>= **Greater than or equal to**. Algebraic comparison and padding are performed.

¬< **Not less than**. (The symbol "¬" may not be found on all keyboards.) Algebraic comparison and padding are performed.

\< **Not less than**. Algebraic comparison and padding are performed.

<= **Less than or equal to**. Algebraic comparison and padding are performed.

¬> **Not greater than**. (The symbol "¬" may not be found on all keyboards.) Algebraic comparison and padding are performed.

\> **Not greater than**. Algebraic comparison and padding are performed.

== **Strictly equal on a character-by-character basis**. No algebraic comparison or padding is done.

¬== **Strictly not equal**, the negation of "==." (The symbol "¬" may not be found on all keyboards.) No algebraic comparison or padding is done.

\== **Strictly not equal**, the negation of "==". No algebraic comparison or padding is done.

>> **Strictly greater than**. No algebraic comparison or padding is done.

>>= **Strictly greater than or equal to**. No algebraic comparison or padding is done.

<< **Strictly less than**. No algebraic comparison or padding is done.

<<= **Strictly less than or equal to**. No algebraic comparison or padding is done.

¬>> **Strictly not greater than**. (The symbol "¬" may not be found on all keyboards.) No algebraic comparison or padding is done.

¬<< **Strictly not less than**. (The symbol "¬" may not be found on all keyboards.) No algebraic comparison or padding is done.

Expression may use one of these comparison connectors:

& **And**. The conditions on both sides of this must be true.

| **Or**. One or both of the conditions on either side of this must be true.

&& **Exclusive Or**. Only one of the conditions on either side of this must be true.

Examples:

```
IF A = 1
THEN SAY "A IS EQUAL TO 1"
ELSE SAY "IT IS NOT"

IF A = 1
THEN
  DO
   SAY "A IS EQUAL TO 1"
   SAY "DO YOU AGREE?"
  END
ELSE
  DO
   SAY "IT IS NOT"
   SAY "WHAT DO YOU THINK?"
  END
```

```
IF REPLY == "YES"
THEN
  DO
   SAY "YOUR REPLY REALLY IS A YES"
  END
ELSE
  DO
   SAY "IT REALLY IS NOT"
  END

IF DAY_OF_WEEK = "FRIDAY" & TEMP > 90
THEN SAY "HEAD FOR THE BEACH"
ELSE SAY "HEAD FOR THE SLOPES"
```

INDEX Function

SAY INDEX(*string, find string*)
Finds *find string* within *string*. If not found, returns a 0. If
found, returns the character position of *find string* within *string*.
Example:

```
SAY INDEX('is there a needle in the haystack?','needle')
   /* 12 */
```

INSERT Function

NEW_STRING = INSERT(*string1, string2, position*)
Inserts *string1* into *string2* after character *position*.
Example:

```
SAY INSERT('E','ABCDF',4)          /* ABCDEF  */
```

INTERPRET Instruction

INTERPRET *string* or *variable*
Causes REXX to look at data (a *string* or the contents of a *variable*) as if it were a line of your program and it was seeing it for the first time.
The data may be a REXX instruction or a command intended for the operating system.
Examples:

```
INTERPRET "SAY 'HI' "

PART1 = "S"
PART2 = "ay 'Hello' "
INTERPRET PART1 || PART2
```

ITERATE Instruction

ITERATE
Within a DO END sequence, sends control to the DO, skipping the instructions between the ITERATE and END. ITERATE goes to the DO of the loop it is in.
If it is in the innermost loop, it goes only to the innermost loop's DO.
Examples:

```
DO I = 1 TO 20
  IF I = 13 THEN ITERATE /* to avoid scaring the superstitious
    */
  SAY I
END

DO 20
    DO I = 1 TO 20
      IF I = 13 THEN ITERATE /* goes to DO on preceding line*/
      SAY I
    END
END
```

ITERATE *variable*
If ITERATE is found in a loop that steps through a *variable*,
ITERATE may reference that variable. This makes REXX check
to be sure the ITERATE is in the correct loop, and control
leaves that loop.
Example:

```
DO I = 1 TO 20
  IF I = 13 THEN ITERATE I
  SAY I
END
```

JUSTIFY Function

SAY JUSTIFY(*string, length*)
Creates a new string from string of length characters. Justifies
to both margins by adding blanks between words.
Example:

```
SAY JUSTIFY('Good morning', 20)     /*Good    morning */
```

SAY JUSTIFY(*string, length,pad*)
Creates a new string from string of length characters.
Justifies to both margins by adding blanks between words.
Uses *pad* as a fill-in character.
The default pad character is a space, as in the
previous example.
Example:

```
SAY JUSTIFY('Good morning', 20,"!")
    /*Good!!!!!!!!!morning */
```

LASTPOS Function

SAY LASTPOS(*string1, string2*)
Finds the last occurrence of *string1* in *string2*.
Returns the character position of the last occurrence.
Returns a 0 if it is not found.
Examples:

```
SAY LASTPOS('left','left right left')  /* 12 */

SAY LASTPOS('center','left right left')/* 0 */
```

SAY LASTPOS(*string1, string2, position*)
Finds the last occurrence of *string1* in *string2* starting
at *position*.
The search proceeds from *position* to the left.
Returns the character position of the last occurrence.
Returns a 0 if it is not found.
If position is omitted, the search begins at the end, as in the
previous two examples.
Example:

```
SAY LASTPOS('left','left right left',5)  /* 1 */
```

LEAVE Instruction

LEAVE
Within a DO END sequence, sends control to the statement
after the END, thus terminating the loop in an orderly fashion.
LEAVE ends the loop it is in.
If it is in the innermost loop, it leaves only the innermost loop.
Example:

```
DO FOREVER
   IF TIME() > "16:00:00" THEN LEAVE
END
```

LEAVE *variable*
If LEAVE is found in a loop that steps through a *variable*,
LEAVE may reference that variable.
This makes REXX check to be sure the LEAVE is in the
correct loop, and control leaves that loop.
Example:

```
DO I = 1 TO 100000
   IF TIME() > "16:00:00" THEN LEAVE I
END
```

LEFT Function

SAY LEFT(*string, length*)
Extracts *length* characters from *string* starting at the left.
Example:

```
SAY LEFT('ABCDEF',3)                 /* ABC */

/* a way to force a variable to a specific length,
padding with blanks or truncating as needed */
REQUIRED_LENGTH = 10 /* for example */
THEVAR = LEFT(THEVAR,REQUIRED_LENGTH)
```

SAY LEFT(*string, length, pad*)
Extracts *length* characters from *string* starting at the left.
Uses *pad* as a fill character if *length* is more than the number
of characters in *string*.
Example:

```
SAY LEFT('ABCDEF',7,'!')             /*ABCDEF! */
```

LENGTH Function

SAY LENGTH(*string*)
Counts the characters in *string*.
Example:

```
SAY LENGTH('ABCDEF')          /* 6 */
```

LINEIN Function (OS/2 and CMS Only)

CALL LINEIN '*file name*'
SAY RESULT

Reads one line from the *file name* specified. Recognizes end of
line, unlike CHARIN.
To tell if end of file has been reached, check LINES('file name')
If it returns a 0, you are at the end of the file.
Examples:

```
/*reads every line in file, one at a time*/
DO WHILE LINES('C:MYFILE.DAT') > 0
  CALL LINEIN 'C:MYFILE.DAT'
  SAY RESULT
END

/*GETS A LINE FROM THE KEYBOARD
AND BYPASSES THE DATA QUEUE*/
CALL LINEIN
SAY RESULT
```

CALL LINEIN '*file name*', *start line, how many*
SAY RESULT

Reads *how many* lines from the *file name* specified, starting
at *start line*.
To tell if end of file has been reached, check LINES('*file name*').
If it returns a 0, you are at the end of the file.

File name may be the name of a data file, or it may be:
    CON:
    KBD:
    COM1: (communications port)
    COM2:
    QUEUE:

LINEOUT Function (OS/2 and CMS Only)

CALL LINEOUT '*file name*', *string*
SAY RESULT

Writes *string* to the *file name* specified.
If the file exists already, it will start at the end of the file and
extend the file.
RESULT contains the number of lines that could not be written;
a 0 indicates a successful write.
Example:

```
CALL LINEOUT 'C:MYFILE.DAT','This is being written'
SAY RESULT (hopefully a 0)
```

CALL LINEOUT '*file name*', *string, start line*
SAY RESULT

Writes *string* to the *file name* specified, starting at *start line*,
overwriting any data that may already exist.
RESULT contains the number of lines that could not be written;
a 0 indicates a successful write.
Example:

```
CALL LINEOUT 'C:MYFILE.DAT','This is being written',1
SAY RESULT (hopefully a 0)
```

CALL LINEOUT '*file name*'　　Closes the file.

File name may be the name of a data file, or it may be:
　　　CON:
　　　PRN:
　　　LPT1:
　　　LPT2:
　　　COM1: (communications port)
　　　COM2:
　　　QUEUE:
　　　STDERR:

LINES Function (OS/2 and CMS Only)

SAY LINES('*file name*')
Tells if any lines remain to be read in *file name.*
If it returns a 0, there are no more lines remaining in the file
so it is at the end of file.
Example:

```
/*reads every line in file, one at a time*/
DO WHILE LINES('C:MYFILE.DAT') > 0
  CALL LINEIN 'C:MYFILE.DAT'
  SAY RESULT /* contains the line just read */
END
```

LISTDSI TSO Only.

RET_CODE = LISTDSI(*dataset name* NORECALL)
　　　or
CALL LISTDSI *dataset name*
RET_CODE = RESULT

Retrieves information about *dataset name* and puts it
into variables:
These variables are set:

SYSDSNAME	the dataset name
SYSVOLUME	volume serial number
SYSUNIT	the unit of the above volume
SYSDSORG	PS: sequential
	PO: partitioned
	DA: direct
	VS: VSAM
SYSRECFM	F: fixed
	V: variable
	B: blocked
	A: ASA printer control
SYSLRECL	Logical record length
SYSBLKSIZE	Block size
SYSKEYLEN	key length
SYSALLOC	space allocation
SYSUSED	space used
SYSPRIMARY	primary space allocation
SYSSECONDS	secondary space allocation
SYSUNITS	space units:
	CYLINDER, TRACK, BLOCK
SYSEXTENTS	space extents used
SYSCREATE	creation date
SYSREFDATE	date of last reference
SYSEXDATE	expiration date
SYSPASSWORD	NONE no password protection
	READ read password required
	WRITE write password required
SYSRACFA	NONE no RACF protection
	GENERIC generic profile exists
	DISCRETE discrete profile exists
SYSUPDATED	YES has been updated
	NO not been updated
SYSTRKSCYL	how many tracks per cylinder
	on the volume
SYSBLKSTRK	how many directory blocks per track
	on the volume

SYSADIRBLK	how many dir blocks allocated
SYSUDIRBLK	how many dir blocks used, if a PDS
SYSMEMBERS	how many members in the PDS
SYSREASON	reason code for command failure
SYSMSGLVL1	first-level error message
SYSMSGLVL2	second-level error message
RET_CODE	0 if it worked, 16 if not
	You may use any other variable besides RET_CODE

Examples:

```
RET_CODE = LISTDSI("ABC.DATA")
SAY SYSLRECL
---> 80
```

```
/* notice apostrophes on next */
RET_CODE = LISTDSI(" 'SYS1.PROCLIB' ")
SAY SYSDSORG
---> PO
```

Reason codes:

0	it worked
1	error occurred in analyzing LISTDSI statement
2	TSO dynamic allocation error
3	cannot process this type of dataset
4	error occurred in obtaining unit name
5	not a catalogued dataset
6	error occurred in obtaining dataset name
7	error occurred in obtaining unit type
8	dataset is not on a disk
9	dataset was migrated by HSM and cannot be recalled
10	unused
11	you do not have authority to obtain directory information
12	this is a VSAM dataset
13	error occurred in opening dataset
14	the device type was not found in MVS tables
15,16	unused
17	abnormal termination occurred

18	information obtained is incomplete
19	this is a multi-volume dataset
20	unknown device type
21	error occurred in catalog search
22	dataset's volume is not mounted
23	I/O error occurred attempting to obtain dataset information
24	dataset is not on this volume
25	dataset was migrated and is not available
26	dataset is on a mass storage device
27	cannot find volume serial number for this dataset
28	the DD name specified is invalid
29	neither dataset name or DD name was specified

NORECALL is optional. It prevents the recall of the dataset from the Hierarchical Storage Manager.

8   MACROS

MACROS, User-written subcommands of the Editor

    TSO

        Member in a PDS/library, just like ordinary REXX program

        Start with usual comment /* REXX anything */

        First operating system command must be ADDRESS ISREDIT "MACRO"

        Default ADDRESS environment is TSO

        To talk to ISPF Editor, you must use ADDRESS ISREDIT "the ISPF Editor command"

        To talk to ISPF, you must use ADDRESS ISPEXEC "the ISPF command"

        See this document for further information:

        http://members.aol.com/rexxauthor/holymac.htm

    CMS

        File Type (second part of file name) must be XEDIT

        Default ADDRESS environment is XEDIT

        To talk to XEDIT, you may simply issue the XEDIT command, in quotes of course

        or you may prefix it with COMMAND: "COMMAND SAVE"

        if it is another macro you are executing,

        you may prefix it with MACRO "MACRO MYPROG"

        To talk to CMS or CP, you may simply issue the CMS or CP command: "PRINT xx xx a1"

        or you may prefix it with CMS: "CMS PRINT xx xx a1"

        or you may use ADDRESS CMS: "the-CMS-command" or "the-CP-command"

        or you may use ADDRESS COMMAND:

        "the-CMS-command" or "CP the-CP-command"

    OS/2

        See the entry on Profile.

REXX Functions   **9**
From MAKEBUF to PARSE

MAKEBUF TSO and CMS Command (TSO and CMS Only)

"MAKEBUF" Creates a new stack or buffer, for your use.
The buffer's number is returned in the variable RC.
It is recommended that you delete the stacks you create,
with DROPBUF.
When you delete a stack with DROPBUF, any data left in it is
no longer available.
Examples:

```
/* try this on your system */
/* MAKEBUF/DROPBUF allows you to create a stack,
   use it, then delete contents of stack     */
"MAKEBUF"                /* create new stack */
BUFNO = RC               /* save stack's number */
PUSH "CART"              /* put something into new stack */
SAY QUEUED()             /* gives a 1 */
"DROPBUF" BUFNO          /* delete stack, and word CART */
SAY QUEUED()             /* gives a 0 */
SAY "ENTER YOUR NAME "   /* talk to terminal */
PULL NAME                /* gets from terminal */
SAY "THANK YOU, " NAME   /* displays "MOE" (perhaps) */
SAY QUEUED()             /* gives a 0 */
SAY "ENTER VEHICLE "
PULL VEHICLE             /* type in TAXI at terminal */
SAY "VEHICLE WAS " VEHICLE /* displays TAXI */
```

```
/* try this on your system */
/* MAKEBUF does not isolate previous stack */
PUSH "CART"                 /* put something into new stack */
SAY QUEUED()                /* gives a 1 */
"MAKEBUF"                   /* create new stack */
BUFNO = RC                  /* save stack's number */
SAY QUEUED()                /* gives a 1 */
SAY "ENTER YOUR NAME "      /* talk to terminal */
PULL NAME                   /* gets from stack */
SAY QUEUED()                /* gives a 0 */
SAY "THANK YOU, " NAME      /* displays CART */
"DROPBUF" BUFNO             /* delete stack */
SAY QUEUED()                /* gives a 0 */
SAY "ENTER VEHICLE "
PULL VEHICLE                /* type in TAXI at terminal */
SAY "VEHICLE WAS " VEHICLE  /* displays TAXI */
```

MAX Function

SAY MAX(*number1, number2, number20*)
Returns the highest of *numbers 1 through 20*.
Example:

```
SAY MAX(5,4,3,2)        /* 5 */
```

MIN Function

SAY MIN(*number1, number2, number20*)
Returns the lowest of *numbers 1 through 20*.
Example:

```
SAY MIN(5,4,3,2)        /* 2 */
```

MSG Function (TSO Only)

SAY MSG()
Returns the current setting of MSG, whether or not TSO
command messages are displayed. Returns either ON
(the default) or OFF.
Example:

```
SAY MSG()          /* ON */
```

MESSAGE_SETTING = MSG("ON" or "OFF")
Returns the current setting of MSG: ON if TSO command
messages are displayed and OFF if not.
A value in the parentheses changes the setting to
that value.
A setting of "OFF" hides error messages from TSO
commands, as when deleting a file that doesn't exist.

Example:

```
MESSAGE_SETTING = MSG("OFF") /* value was on. turn it off */
SAY MSG()                    /* OFF  now it's off */
SAY MESSAGE_SETTING          /* ON but it was on */
```

NEWSTACK TSO Command (TSO Only)

"NEWSTACK"
This TSO command creates a new stack for immediate use
within your REXX program. Anything that may have been in
the old stack is unavailable. It can be neither read, nor
changed.
Keep track of how many new stacks you create and be sure to
execute the DELSTACK command once for each new stack to
eliminate them.
Please see the QSTACK instruction for information on how to
facilitate this.
When you do a DELSTACK, the old stack is again available
for use.

Examples:

```
/* try this on your system */
/* NEWSTACK isolates previous stack
   DELSTACK allows you to go back to previous stack */
PUSH "CART"                 /* put something into new stack */
SAY QUEUED()                /* gives a 1 */
"NEWSTACK"                  /* create new stack, isolate old */
SAY QUEUED()                /* gives a 0 */
SAY "ENTER YOUR NAME "      /* talk to terminal */
PULL NAME                   /* gets from terminal */
SAY QUEUED()                /* gives a 0 */
SAY "THANK YOU, " NAME      /* displays "MOE" (perhaps)*/
"DELSTACK"                  /* goes back to old stack */
SAY QUEUED()                /* gives a 1 */
SAY "ENTER VEHICLE "
PULL VEHICLE                /* gets from stack (you don't type in)*/
SAY "VEHICLE WAS " VEHICLE  /* displays CART */


/* try this on your system */
/* NEWSTACK isolates previous stack
   DELSTACK allows you to go back to previous stack */
"NEWSTACK"                  /* create new stack, isolate old */
PUSH "CART"                 /* put something into new stack */
SAY QUEUED()                /* gives a 1 */
"DELSTACK"                  /* goes back to old stack */
SAY QUEUED()                /* gives a 0 */
SAY "ENTER YOUR NAME "      /* talk to terminal */
PULL NAME                   /* gets from terminal */
SAY QUEUED()                /* gives a 0 */
SAY "THANK YOU, " NAME      /* displays "MOE" (perhaps) */
SAY QUEUED()                /* gives a 1 */
SAY "ENTER VEHICLE "
PULL VEHICLE                /* type in TAXI at terminal */
SAY "VEHICLE WAS " VEHICLE  /* displays TAXI */
```

NOP Instruction

NOP
Null instruction that does nothing.
Used afterTHEN, ELSE or OTHERWISE when no action is
to be taken.
Example:

```
IF A = B THEN NOP
ELSE SAY "SORRY A IS NOT EQUAL TO B"
```

NUMERIC Instruction

NUMERIC *option*
Sets the way numbers are handled in arithmetic operations
and comparisons.

Options: (explained below)

DIGITS
FORM
FUZZ

NUMERIC DIGITS *number*
Sets the precision of arithmetic operations.
Causes REXX to use *number* digits in arithmetic operations
(but not in built-in functions.)
The system default is 9.
Use this instruction if you need more or less.
You may use from 1 to (perhaps) 20000.
There is a high overhead with large precision.
Rounding is performed when an arithmetic operation
produces more digits than *number*.

NUMERIC FORM SCIENTIFIC or ENGINEERING
Sets the way large numbers are shown in exponential notation
Examples:

```
NUMERIC FORM SCIENTIFIC (the default)
SAY 1.0001 * 100000000000   /* 1.00010000E+11 */

NUMERIC FORM ENGINEERING
SAY 1.0001 * 100000000000   /* 100.010000E+9 */
```

NUMERIC FUZZ *number*
Controls the number of low order digits ignored in numeric
comparisons. Allows approximations instead of strict equality.
Example:

```
NUMERIC FUZZ 1
IF 987654321 = 987654322
THEN SAY "SURPRISE"
ELSE SAY "THIS WON'T HAPPEN"
```

OPTIONS

OPTIONS *choice*

choice may be:

ETMODE	literal strings may contain double byte characters, which are checked for validity
NOETMODE	(the default) literal strings may contain double byte characters which are not checked for validity
EXMODE	double byte characters in literal strings are to be handled on a logical character basis so that DBCS data integrity is maintained
NOEXMODE	(the default) double byte characters in literal strings are to be handled on a byte basis so that the integrity of DBCS data is not guaranteed

OTHERWISE keyword of the SELECT Instruction
introduces the default alternative in the SELECT structure, the
path that is taken if no other alternative is true.
OTHERWISE is not required after a SELECT.
An END is required at the very end of the SELECT structure,
whether or not there is an OTHERWISE.

Examples:

```
SELECT
  WHEN DAY = 1 THEN  SAY  "MONDAY"
  WHEN DAY = 2 THEN  SAY  "TUESDAY"
  WHEN DAY = 3 THEN  SAY  "WEDNESDAY"
  WHEN DAY = 4 THEN  SAY  "THURSDAY"
  WHEN DAY = 5 THEN  SAY  "FRIDAY"
  WHEN DAY = 6 THEN  SAY  "SATURDAY"
  WHEN DAY = 7 THEN  SAY  "SUNDAY"
OTHERWISE
  DO /* recommended for OTHERWISE */
    SAY "ARE YOU ON MARS?"
  END /* recommended for OTHERWISE */
END /* required for the SELECT */
```

OUTTRAP Function (TSO Only)

CALL OUTTRAP "*stem.*", *how many lines*
Turns on capturing of the display output of TSO commands, such as "LISTCAT," "LISTDS," error messages as from "DELETE DOESNT.EXIST," SAY in another EXEC, or a WRITE in a CLIST. Each line of output is captured in a different element of the array created from *stem.*
A maximum of *how many lines* will be captured, with "*" meaning "capture all lines."
Returns:

stem.0   contains the number of lines produced
stem.1   contains the first line
stem.2   contains the second line, etc.

Example:

```
CALL OUTTRAP "LINE.", "*"
"LISTDS NO.SUCH.DATASET"
SAY LINE.1    /* DATASET NO.SUCH.DATASET NOT IN CATALOG */
SAY LINE.0    /* 1 */
```

CALL OUTTRAP "OFF"
Turns off the trapping of command output so the commands will resume displaying their output at the terminal.

CALL OUTTRAP "LINE.", "0"
Discards the displayed output of commands such as "LISTCAT," "LISTDS," error messages as from "DELETE DOESNT.EXIST," SAY in another EXEC, or a WRITE in a CLIST. The output is not displayed at the terminal and is not captured.

OVERLAY Function

New_string = OVERLAY(*string1, string2, position*)
Replaces characters in *string2* with characters in *string1*, starting in character *position* of *string2*.
Example:

```
SAY OVERLAY('D','ABCXEF',4)          /* ABCDEF */
```

ARSE Instruction

PARSE [UPPER] *origin template*
Performs character string manipulation according to various
rules that may be specified in the instruction.
Data is taken from *origin* and processed by *template*, with the
final result being that all the variables in the template are
changed or set in some way.
If UPPER is specified, all letters are uppercased; otherwise,
they are left in the case they were in.

Origins:

ARG	the command line
EXTERNAL	(TSO and CMS Only) the terminal without passing through the Data Queue
PULL	the stack or Data Queue
LINEIN	(OS/2 Only) the terminal or monitor without passing through the stack
SOURCE	internal system settings about the environment and the program
VALUE	a literal, function, or possibly a variable
VAR	a variable
VERSION	internal system information about the version of REXX you are using

Templates:

Just variables   Data is distributed into the variables, delimited by spaces.

Example:

```
PARSE UPPER ARG VAR1 VAR2 VAR3
SAY VAR1
SAY VAR2
SAY VAR3
```

/* the following is entered at the command line */
JOHN RINGO PAUL

Results:
         JOHN
         RINGO
         PAUL

Literal string and variables

Data is first split at the position of the literal string and then examined in two parts: the part on the left of the literal string, then the part on the right of the literal string.
Finally it is distributed into the variables, delimited by spaces.
Example:

```
PARSE UPPER ARG VAR1 VAR2 "!" VAR3
SAY VAR1
SAY VAR2
SAY VAR3
```

/* the following is entered at the command line */
John said "Yo! Where are you going?"

Results:
         JOHN
         SAID "YO
         WHERE ARE YOU GOING?"

Column delimiters and variables

Data is first split at the columns specified.

Note: for each variable, the columns that are placed into it may be determined by examining the numbers on either side of it. The number on the left is its starting column, the number on the right, minus 1, is its ending column.

Examples:

```
PARSE UPPER ARG 1 VAR1 4  VAR2 8 VAR3 11
SAY VAR1
SAY VAR2
SAY VAR3
```

```
/* the following is entered at the command line */
ABCDEFGHIJKLMNOPQRSTUVWXYZ
```

Results:
       ABC
       DEFG
       HIJ

```
PARSE UPPER ARG 1 VAR1 4 6 VAR2 8 5  VAR3 11
SAY VAR1
SAY VAR2
SAY VAR3
```

the following is entered at the command line */
BCDEFGHIJKLMNOPQRSTUVWXYZ

Results:
       ABC
       FG
       EFGHIJK

10   Precedence of Operators

PRECEDENCE OF OPERATORS

Prefix operators: + - not symbol   \

Raise to a power: **

Multiplication and division: * / % //

Addition and subtraction: + -

Concatenation: the blank space or spaces, the concatenation operator ||, abuttal, or placing two items next to each other with no intervening spaces.

Comparison operators: = == > < >= <= <> and the others (see under comparison operators)

Logical and: &

Logical or: | &&

A term bracketed by parentheses: the items inside of parentheses are evaluated before the term.

Left to right

REXX Functions 11
From POS to X2D

OS Function

SAY POS(*string1, string2, start pos*)
Returns the position of *string1* in *string2*.
Returns 0 if *string1* is not in *string2*.
Begins its search at *start pos*.
If *start pos* is absent, the search begins at the first character.
Example:

```
SAY POS('DEF','ABCDEFGHIJKLMNOP',1)    /* 4 */
```

ROCEDURE Instruction

subroutine: PROCEDURE
Used in an internal function/subroutine named *subroutine* to
protect the variables of the main part of the program from
any possible change, and even from being examined, by the
function/subroutine.
Makes all variables in the function/subroutine local.
Example:

```
SUBR1:  PROCEDURE
```

PROFILE.ERX (OS/2 Only)
OS/2 Enhanced editor macro/profile that you can copy and use.

```
/* REXX enhanced editor profile
   place in the directory C:\OS2\APPS\ with the name PROFILE.EI
  turns off the automatic supplying of End for DO, ELSE for IF, e
   also switches to constant spacing type face
  after storing it in the proper directory, go into the enhance
        editor and open click on Command, then type in PROFILE ON
        press ENTER,click on Options, click on Save Options
*/
"EXPAND OFF"
"MONOFONT"
```

PROMPT Function (TSO Only)

SAY PROMPT()
Returns the current setting of PROMPT, whether or not TSO
commands can prompt. Returns ON or OFF (the default)
Example:

```
SAY PROMPT()           /* OFF */
```

PROMPT_SETTING = PROMPT("ON" or "OFF")
Returns the current setting of PROMPT, ON if TSO command:
can prompt, OFF if they can not.
It stores it in a variable, and changes the setting to the value ir
the parentheses.
Example:

```
SAY PROMPT()                     /* OFF it is off now */
PROMPT_SETTING = PROMPT("ON") /* it was off, turn it on*/
"PROFILE PROMPT"                 /* be sure TSO allows prompting */
SAY PROMPT()                     /* ON it is on now */
SAY PROMPT_SETTING               /* OFF but it was off */
```

ULL Instruction

hort form of PARSE UPPER PULL. Takes a line from the stack or,
it is empty, from the terminal or keyboard.
    See PARSE UPPER PULL.

USH Instruction

PUSH *string* or *variable*
Puts a line consisting of *variable*, or *string* into the stack.
Data is put into the stack LIFO.
Example:

```
PUSH "HAS FLEAS"
PUSH "MY DOG"
PULL LINE
SAY LINE
PULL LINE
SAY LINE
```

BUF TSO and CMS Command (TSO and CMS Only)

"QBUF"
this environment command tells you how many buffers were
created by MAKEBUF.
The number of buffers is returned in the special variable RC.
Examples:

```
"QBUF"
SAY RC /* gives a 0 */
"MAKEBUF"
"QBUF"
SAY RC /* gives a 1 */
"DROPBUF"
"QBUF"
SAY RC /* gives a 0 */
```

QELEM TSO and CMS Command (TSO and CMS Only)

"QELEM"

This environment command tells you how many elements or lines are available in the buffer created by MAKEBUF.
The number of elements is returned in the special variable RC.
Examples:

```
"MAKEBUF"
PUSH "CART"
PUSH "CAR"
"QELEM"
SAY RC              /* 2 */
"DROPBUF"
"QELEM"
SAY RC              /* 0 */
```

QSTACK TSO Command (TSO Only)

This TSO command tells you how many stacks you have created by using "NEWSTACK"
It places the number of stacks you have created by using "NEWSTACK" (plus one) into the special variable RC.
You may use RC (minus one) to determine how many times to execute "DELSTACK."

Example:

```
"QSTACK"
HOW_MANY = RC - 1
DO HOW_MANY
   "DELSTACK"
END
```

QUEUE Instruction

QUEUE *string* or *variable*
Puts a line consisting of *variable* or *string* into the stack (internal Data Queue). Data is put into the stack FIFO.
Examples:

```
QUEUE "MY DOG"
QUEUE "HAS FLEAS"
PULL LINE
SAY LINE
PULL LINE
SAY LINE
```

QUEUED Function

SAY QUEUED()
Returns the number of lines in the stack (internal Data Queue).
Example:

```
SAY QUEUED()          /* 0 */
PUSH 'CART'
SAY QUEUED()          /* 1 */
```

RANDOM

SAY RANDOM(*min, max*)
Returns a random number between *min* and *max*.
Example:

```
SAY RANDOM(1,100)              /* 55 (perhaps) */
```

SAY RANDOM(*min, max, seed*)

Returns a random number between *min* and *max*.
Specifying the same *seed* produces the same series each
time on all systems that REXX is found on.
Examples:

```
SAY RANDOM(1,100,12345)              /* 5 */
SAY RANDOM(1,100,12345)              /* 5 */
SAY RANDOM(1,100)                    /* 75 */
SAY RANDOM(1,100)                    /* 21 */
SAY RANDOM(1,100)                    /* 57 */
```

RC Reserved variable

Contains the return code that was set by an environment command.
If the command functions properly, this normally contains a 0.
There are exceptions, however: see MAKEBUF, QELEM, QBUF.
It also contains the number assigned to REXX syntax errors.
It is not set by REXX verbs or instructions such as IF, CALL, etc.
   Examples:

```
SIGNAL ON SYNTAX
SAY "A" - "B"
EXIT
SYNTAX:
SAY RC " IS THE REXX ERROR NUMBER"
SAY ERRORTEXT(RC) " IS THE TEXT OF THE ERROR MES-
   SAGE "
EXIT

"MAKEBUF"
SAY RC /* returns a 1 or greater */

"DELETE ABC.DATA" /* on TSO */
SAY RC /* a 0, if the delete worked */

"ERASE ABC.DAT" /* on OS/2 */
SAY RC /* a 0, if the erase worked */

"ERASE ABC DATA" /* on CMS */
SAY RC /* a 0, if the erase worked */
```

RESULT Reserved Variable

Contains the result or answer passed back by a function or subroutine that was invoked with a REXX CALL.

It will contain the string or variable that was found on the function's or subroutine's RETURN statement.

The function or subroutine may be built in, user-written internal, or user-written external.

Examples:

```
SAY RESULT      /* gives RESULT, since RESULT not yet set */
CALL LENGTH "ABCD"
SAY RESULT      /* 4 */
EXIT

CALL ADDEMUP 1, 2
SAY RESULT      /* 3 */
EXIT
ADDEMUP:
ARG NUMBER1, NUMBER2
RETURN  NUMBER1 + NUMBER2
```

RETURN Instruction

RETURN *string* or *variable*
In a function/subroutine, sends control back to the instruction after the one that invoked the function/subroutine.
Passes back *string* or *variable* to the caller, except in an error trap, where nothing is passed back.
Example:

```
SUBR:
ARG NUM1,NUM2
TOTAL = NUM1 + NUM2
RETURN TOTAL
```

If no function or subroutine is active, that is that control has reached the RETURN through a SIGNAL or by dropping through, RETURN terminates the program like EXIT.
Any character format string contained on the RETURN instruction will cause an data conversion or datatype error, because only numerics (or nothing) may be specified when ending the program.
Example that will produce an error:

```
Signal Date_Time    /* go to the subroutine */
Exit                /* never get here */
Date_Time:          /* the subroutine */
Return Date() Time()
/* return acts like an EXIT.
  EXIT is not allowed to pass character strings
  to the operating system.
  The operating system displays an error message.*/
```

REVERSE Function

SAY REVERSE(*string*)
Reverses the characters of the *string*.
Example:

```
SAY REVERSE('GO')                        /* OG */
```

RIGHT Function

SAY RIGHT(*string, length*)
Extracts *length* characters from *string* starting at the right.
Example:

```
SAY RIGHT('ABCDEF',3)        /* DEF */
```

SAY RIGHT(*string, length, pad*)
Extracts *length* characters from *string* starting at the right.
Uses *pad* as a fill character if *length* is more than the number
of characters in *string*.
Examples:

```
SAY RIGHT('ABCDEF',7,'!')           /* !ABCDEF */
```

RT TSO and CMS Command (TSO and CMS Only)
Resumes display to the terminal that was stopped by the
command HT.

- On TSO, it may be executed after an attention interrupt
obtained by pressing the PA1 key or the ATTN key.

- On CMS, it may be executed as a CMS immediate command
when the screen is displaying MORE . . . in the lower right.

RXFUNCADD Function (OS/2 only)
You are most likely to use this function for one purpose only: registering certain other functions with REXX.
(This is conceptually like loading them into memory where they are available for use.)
Those functions are not useable until you do this.
What you have to do is very simple: put program statements similar to those shown just below
in each program that uses one of the REXX functions that require pre-registering.

```
/* Showload.CMD */
/* shows how to register a function with OS/2
so that you can use it in your program

change "syscls" shown below to the function name
that you are actually using
*/

Function_to_load = "syscls"
Call rxfuncadd function_to_load,'rexxutil',
    function_to_load
/* now you can use the function in this program*/
CALL SYSCLS
Say "SYSCLS has been loaded"
```

Here is a list of the functions that won't work unless you register them with the program statements shown above.

RXMESSAGEBOX
SYSCLS
SYSCREATEOBJECT
SYSCURPOS
SYSCURSTATE
SYSDEREGISTEROBJECTCLASS
SYSDESTROYOBJECT
SYSDRIVEINFO
SYSDRIVEMAP
SYSDROPFUNCS
SYSFILEDELETE
SYSFILETREE

SYSFILESEARCH
SYSGETEA
SYSGETKEY
SYSGETMESSAGE
SYSINI (not covered here)
SYSMKDIR
SYSOS2VER
SYSPUTEA
SYSQUEUECLASSLIST
SYSREGISTEROBJECTCLASS
SYSRMDIR
SYSSEARCHPATH
SYSSETICON
SYSSETOBJECTDATA
SYSSLEEP
SYSTEMPFILENAME
SYSTEXTSCREENREAD
SYSTEXTSCREENSIZE
SYSWAITNAMEDPIPE

RXMESSAGEBOX Function (OS/2 Only)

CALL RXMESSAGEBOX *'text'*, *'title'*, *'button'*, *'icon'*
SAY 'CODE FOR KEY PRESSED WAS' RESULT

Displays a Presentation Manager message box where the
message *text* figures prominently with *title* at the top.
A *button* is included in the box as well as an *icon*.
Requires pre-registering, discussed under RXFUNCADD
in this book.
Can only be used under the Presentation Manager.
This means you must execute your program by putting the
word PMREXX in front of it, as for example: PMREXX MYPROG.

button may be:

OK	An OK button (the default)
OKCANCEL	An OK button and a CANCEL button
CANCEL	A CANCEL button
ENTER	An ENTER button
ENTERCANCEL	An ENTER button and a CANCEL button
RETRYCANCEL	A RETRY button and a CANCEL button
ABORTRETRYCANCEL	An ABORT button, a RETRY button and a CANCEL button.
YESNO	A YES button and a NO button.
YESNOCANCEL	A YES button, a NO button, and a CANCEL button.

icon may be one of the following types

NONE	No icon is displayed.
HAND	
QUESTION	
EXCLAMATION	
ASTERISK	
INFORMATION	
QUERY	
WARNING	
ERROR	

RESULT contains a number corresponding to the key
that was pressed.

1   OK
2   CANCEL
3   ABORT
4   RETRY
5   IGNORE
6   YES
7   NO
8   ENTER

Example:

```
CALL RXMESSAGEBOX 'OK to continue?', 'Sample message box',,
  'YESNO', 'QUESTION'
IF RESULT = 6
THEN SAY 'THANK YOU FOR PRESSING YES'
```

RXQUEUE Function (OS/2 Only)

CALL RXQUEUE *'action','queue name'*
SAY RESULT

Creates and deletes Data Queues, makes them available for
use, and queries their names.

action
GET	gives the name of the queue currently in use
SET	sets a queue (makes it the current one)
DELETE	deletes the queue (you must explicitly delete it)
CREATE	creates a queue (if it already exists, one is created with a different name that is available in RESULT)

CALL RXQUEUE 'GET'
SAY RESULT

The name of the current queue is given in RESULT. SESSION is the name of the default queue created automatically by REXX. Example:

```
CALL RXQUEUE 'GET'
SAY THE CURRENT QUEUE IS' RESULT
```

CALL RXQUEUE 'CREATE', 'queue name'
SAY RESULT

Creates a queue named *queue name.*
If *queue name* already exists one is created with a name chosen by REXX and available in RESULT.
In order to use the queue you have created you need to do a set (see below).
Example:

```
CALL RXQUEUE CREATE', 'MYQUEUE'
SAY 'CREATED QUEUE' RESULT
```

CALL RXQUEUE 'SET', *'queue name'*
SAY RESULT

Makes the queue named *queue name* the current one.
The name of the old queue is available in RESULT.
You must have already created the queue in order to use it.
Example:

```
CALL RXQUEUE 'SET', 'MYQUEUE'
SAY 'THE PREVIOUS QUEUE WAS' RESULT
```

CALL RXQUEUE 'DELETE', '*queue name*'
SAY RESULT

Deletes the queue named *queue name.*
If you don't delete it, it will continue to exist until you do,
outlasting sessions, windows, and bootings.
If the delete is successful, RESULT will contain a zero (0).
Example:

```
CALL RXQUEUE 'DELETE', 'MYQUEUE'
IF RESULT = 0
THEN SAY 'DELETED THE QUEUE'
```

SAY Instruction

SAY *string* or *variable*
Displays a line on the terminal or monitor, consisting of *string*
or *variable.*
Examples:

```
SAY "AAAAAHHH"

A = 1
SAY A
```

SELECT Instruction

REXX's implementation of the CASE structure.
Allows selection of just one of several possible alternatives.
An END is required at the very end of the structure, whether
an OTHERWISE is used or not.

Example:

```
SELECT
  WHEN DAY = 1 THEN SAY "MONDAY"
  WHEN DAY = 2 THEN SAY "TUESDAY"
  WHEN DAY = 3 THEN SAY "WEDNESDAY"
  WHEN DAY = 4 THEN SAY "THURSDAY"
  WHEN DAY = 5 THEN SAY "FRIDAY"
  WHEN DAY = 6 THEN SAY "SATURDAY"
  WHEN DAY = 7 THEN SAY "SUNDAY"
END /* required for SELECT */


SELECT
  WHEN DAY = 1 THEN SAY "MONDAY"
  WHEN DAY = 2 THEN SAY "TUESDAY"
  WHEN DAY = 3 THEN SAY "WEDNESDAY"
  WHEN DAY = 4 THEN SAY "THURSDAY"
  WHEN DAY = 5 THEN SAY "FRIDAY"
  WHEN DAY = 6 THEN SAY "SATURDAY"
  WHEN DAY = 7 THEN SAY "SUNDAY"
OTHERWISE
  DO /* recommended for OTHERWISE */
    SAY "ARE YOU ON MARS?"
    SAY "OR IS IT VENUS?"
  END /* recommended for OTHERWISE */
END /* required for SELECT */
```

SETLOCAL Function (OS/2 Only)

CALL SETLOCAL
SAY RESULT

Saves the drive directory and environment variables
that are in effect.
A 1 is returned in RESULT if the function was successful;
a 0 is returned if it was not successful.
Example:

```
CALL SETLOCAL
SAY RESULT
```

SETLOCAL Instruction (OS/2 Only)
Saves the current working drive and directory.
The ENDLOCAL command can restore them.

SIGL Reserved Variable
Contains the line number of the REXX program statement that
caused a transfer of control into a subroutine or condition trap.
This is very useful in debugging a program.
Example:

```
SIGNAL ON SYNTAX
SAY "A" - "B"
EXIT
SYNTAX:
SAY SIGL " IS THE LINE NUMBER WITH THE ERROR"
EXIT
```

SIGN Function

SAY SIGN(*number*)
Returns 1 if *number* is positive, 0 if it is zero and -1 if it is negative.
Example:

```
SAY SIGN(-9)                /* -1 */
```

SIGNAL Instruction

SIGNAL ON or OFF *label*
Turns on or off a condition trap named by *label*.
The condition trap can intercept an exceptional condition
whenever it occurs after that.
The condition trap is physically located at the end of
the program.

Labels:

SYNTAX	REXX syntax error
ERROR	command to environment not correct
FAILURE	command to environment doesn't exist
NOVALUE	uninitialized variable
HALT	attention interrupt
	/* TSO: press PA1 or ATTN
	CMS: type HI when screen
	displays More ... in lower right
	OS/2: press CTRL and C or CTRL
	and Break*/
NOTREADY	(OS/2 Only). Error in input/output

Examples:

```
SIGNAL ON SYNTAX
/*intervening instructions */
EXIT
SYNTAX:
SAY "ENTERED SYNTAX TRAP"
SAY "SYNTAX ERROR IS " ERRORTEXT(RC)
SAY "LINE NUMBER IN ERROR IS " SIGL
SAY "LINE IN ERROR IS " SOURCELINE(SIGL)

SELECT /* OS/2: obtain the complete error msg for REXX errors*/
     /* no space between Rex and "RC */
     WHEN  Address() = "CMD" then" Call Help Rex"RC
     WHEN  Address() = "PMREXX" then" Call Help Rex"RC
END
EXIT
SIGNAL ON ERROR
/*intervening instructions */
EXIT
ERROR:
SAY "ENTERED ERROR TRAP"
```

```
   SAY "RETURN CODE FROM ENVIRONMENT IS " RC
   SAY "LINE NUMBER IN ERROR IS " SIGL
   SAY "LINE IN ERROR IS " SOURCELINE(SIGL)
   SELECT /* OS/2: obtain complete  msg for Command errors*/
       /* no space between Sys and "RC */
       WHEN  Address() = "CMD" then" Call Help Sys"RC
       WHEN  Address() = "PMREXX" then" Call Help Sys"RC
   END
   EXIT
   SIGNAL ON FAILURE
   /*intervening instructions */
   EXIT
   FAILURE:
   SAY "ENTERED FAILURE TRAP"
   SAY "RETURN CODE FROM ENVIRONMENT IS " RC
   SAY "LINE NUMBER IN ERROR IS " SIGL
   SAY "LINE IN ERROR IS " SOURCELINE(SIGL)
   SELECT /* OS/2: obtain the complete error msg
for Command errors*/
       /* no space between Sys and "RC */
       WHEN  Address() = "CMD" then "Call Help Sys"RC
       WHEN  Address() = "PMREXX" then "Call Help Sys"RC
   END
   EXIT

   SIGNAL ON NOVALUE
   /*intervening instructions */
   EXIT
   NOVALUE:
   SAY "ENTERED NOVALUE TRAP"
   SAY "STRING IN ERROR IS " CONDITION("D")
   SAY "LINE NUMBER IN ERROR IS " SIGL
   SAY "LINE IN ERROR IS " SOURCELINE(SIGL)
   EXIT
```

```
SIGNAL ON HALT
/*intervening instructions */
EXIT
HALT:
SAY "ENTERED HALT TRAP"
SAY "ABOUT TO TERMINATE PROGRAM"
SAY "PRESS ENTER TO PROCEED"
PULL .
EXIT
SIGNAL ON NOTREADY
/*intervening instructions */
EXIT
NOTREADY:
SAY "ENTERED NOTREADY TRAP"
SAY "LINE NUMBER IN ERROR IS " SIGL
SAY "LINE IN ERROR IS " SOURCELINE(SIGL)
EXIT
```

SIGNAL *label*
SIGNAL followed by *label* is an unconditional "GO TO."
This should be used with caution because its use will interfere
with REXX's control structures such as DO . . . END.

SOURCELINE Function

SAY SOURCELINE(*number*)
Returns original program statement with line number *number.*
Example:

```
/*REXX PROGRAM TO SHOW SOURCELINE*/
SAY SOURCELINE(1)          /*REXX PROGRAM TO SHOW SOURCELINE*/
```

SAY SOURCELINE()

Returns number of lines in the program.
Examples:

```
/*REXX PROGRAM TO SHOW SOURCELINE*/
SAY SOURCELINE() /* 2 */

DO I = 1 TO SOURCELINE() /* displays entire program
  */
  SAY SOURCELINE(I)
END
/* or do it this way in interactive debug */
DO I = 1 TO SOURCELINE() ; SAY SOURCELINE(I); END
```

SPACE Function

SAY SPACE(*string, how many blanks*)

Puts *how many blanks* blanks between words in *string*.
If *how many blanks* is 0, strips blanks in *string*.
Examples:

```
SAY SPACE('THE FINAL FRONTIER',3)/* THE  FINAL  FRONTIER */

SAY SPACE('DONT SPACE  OUT ON ME',0)/* DONTSPACEOUTONME */
```

SAY SPACE(*string, how many pad char, pad*)

Moves apart the words in *string* and puts *how many pad char*
copies of *pad* between the words.
If *how many pad char* is 0, strips blanks in *string*.
Examples:

```
SAY SPACE('THE FINAL FRONTIER',3,'!')/* THE!!!FINAL!!!FRONTIER */

SAY SPACE('DONT SPACE  OUT ON ME',0,'!')   /* DONTSPACEOUTONME */
```

STORAGE Function (TSO and CMS Only)

SAY STORAGE(*address, length*)

Retrieves the actual contents of memory (storage) that is at
address address.
Example:

```
SAY STORAGE(000000,8) /* ??????? */
```

CALL STORAGE *address, length, new data*

Stores *new data* at the memory address *address*, overlaying
the previous contents of memory for a length of *length*.
Use at your own risk.

STREAM Function (OS/2 and CMS Only)

CALL STREAM '*file name*', 'C', '*command*'
SAY RESULT

Performs the action indicated by *command* on *file name*.
RESULT indicates the success or failure.
If the command succeeded, RESULT will contain the name of
the command. If the command failed, RESULT will contain an
error message.

Commands:

QUERY EXISTS	Returns file name if OK; otherwise null.
QUERY SIZE	Returns the size in bytes.
QUERY DATETIME	Returns date and time stamps.
OPEN READ	Returns READY: if OK. Note the colon.
OPEN WRITE	Returns READY: if OK. Note the colon.
CLOSE	Returns READY: if OK. Note the colon.
SEEK *offset*	Sets the READ or WRITE position *offset* bytes from the beginning of the file. you may include an operator, example: SEEK = 123
=	set offset this many bytes from the beginning of the file
<	set offset this many bytes from the end of the file
+	set offset this many bytes forward from the current position
-	set offset this many bytes backward from the current position

Another way to close a file: Call lineout file_name
Another way to open a file: (if already open, a NOP) Call linein file_name ,,0

CALL STREAM 'C:MYFILE.DAT', 'C', 'CLOSE' Closes the file.

IF STREAM('TMP.DAT','C','QUERY EXISTS') = ""
THEN SAY 'THE FILE DOES NOT EXIST'
ELSE SAY 'THE FILE EXISTS'

An excellent way to determine if a file exists or not.

CALL STREAM '*file name*', 'S'
SAY RESULT

Finds out the status of *file name*. RESULT contains the current status.

Values of RESULT:

ERROR
NOTREADY
READY (ready for reading/writing; READY is without a colon)
UNKNOWN (indicates closed status or no such file)

CALL STREAM '*file name*', 'S'
SAY RESULT

Returns the State of the file. RESULT contains one of the following:

Values of RESULT:

ERROR	you are trying to do something illegal
NOTREADY	something is preventing you from reading or writing the file, for example it doesn't exist or you have already reached the end of the file.
READY	the file exists and is ready for reading or writing.
Unknown	this may mean that the file hasn't been opened yet

STRIP Function

NEW_STRING = STRIP(*string, option*)
Strips blanks from *string* based on *option*:
Options:

B — remove both leading and trailing blanks (default)
T — remove trailing blanks
L — remove leading blanks

Example:

```
NEW_STRING = STRIP('   MUCH BLANK SPACE   ')
SAY NEW_STRING   /* MUCH BLANK SPACE */
```

NEW_STRING = STRIP(*string, option, character*)
Strips *character* from *string* based on *option*:

Options:
B — remove both leading and trailing *character* (default)
T — remove trailing *character*
L — remove leading *character*

Example:

```
NEW_STRING = STRIP('CAFE AU LAIT!!!!','T','!')
SAY NEW_STRING   /* CAFE AU LAIT */
```

SUBCOM TSO and CMS Command (TSO and CMS Only)
This TSO/CMS command asks TSO or CMS if an environment is available for use.
The answer is returned in the special variable RC, which contains a 0 for yes, a 1 for no.
Examples:

```
"SUBCOM" TSO
SAY RC        /* 0 */

"SUBCOM" ISPEXEC
SAY RC        /* 0  (under TSO, only if you are in ISPF) */

"SUBCOM" XEDIT
SAY RC        /* 0 (under CMS, only if you are in XEDIT) */

"SUBCOM" MARS
SAY RC        /* 1 */
```

SUBSTR Function

NEW_STRING = SUBSTR(*string, start position, length*)
Returns a portion of *string* beginning at *start position* for a length of *length*.
Blanks are used if filler characters are needed.
Example:

```
SAY SUBSTR('PACE',2,3)      /* ACE */
```

NEW_STRING = SUBSTR(*string, start position, length,pad*)
Returns a portion of *string* beginning at *start position* for a length of *length*.
Pad is used if filler characters are needed.
Example:

```
SAY SUBSTR('PACE',2,5,'!' )/* ACE!! */
```

SUBWORD Function

NEW_STRING = SUBWORD
(*string, starting word, how many words*)
Returns a portion of *string* beginning at *starting word*, containing *how many words* words.
Examples:

```
NEW_STRING = SUBWORD('ET PHONE HOME COLLECT',2,2)
SAY NEW_STRING   /* PHONE HOME */
```

SYMBOL Function

SAY SYMBOL(*name*)
Tells if *name* is a variable, literal, or if not a legal symbol.

Returns:

VAR   <--- if name is an assigned variable
LIT   <--- if name is a literal
BAD   <---ifnameisnotalegalsymbol

Examples:

```
SAY SYMBOL('*-=:*')                    /* BAD */
TEAM = 'YANKEES'
SAY SYMBOL('YANKEES')                  /* LIT */
SAY SYMBOL('TEAM')                     /* VAR */
```

SYSCLS Function (OS/2 Only)

CALL SYSCLS
Clears the screen.
Does not work properly under Presentation Manager.
Requires pre-registering, discussed under RXFUNCADD
in this book.
Example:

```
CALL SYSCLS
```

SYSCREATEOBJECT Function (OS/2 Only)

CALL SYSCREATEOBJECT *classname, title, location, icon*
SAY RESULT
Creates a new instance of an object class.
The name assigned is *classname, title* is assigned as the
object's title, *location* is the name of the place to put the object
in, or the path to the object's location, *icon* is the name of an
icon file (extension .ICO).
RESULT will contain a 1 if the creation was successful, a 0 if it
was not.
Requires pre-registering, discussed under RXFUNCADD in
this book.
Example:

```
CALL SYSCREATEOBJECT "<WPFolder>",,      <- object class
                  'This is my Folder',, <- title
                  '<WP_DESKTOP>",,, <-location of new object
                  "myicon.ICO" <- icon
```

SYSCURPOS Function (OS/2 Only)

CALL SYSCURPOS
SAY RESULT

Will not work under the Presentation Manager.
Tells the current cursor position.
The cursor position is returned in RESULT.
It consists of two numbers, row and column.
Requires pre-registering, discussed under RXFUNCADD in
this book.
Example:

```
CALL SYSCURPOS
PARSE VAR RESULT ROW COLUMN
SAY 'CURSOR IS AT ROW' ROW 'COLUMN' COLUMN
```

CALL SYSCURPOS *row, column*
SAY RESULT

Will not work under the Presentation Manager.
Moves the cursor to *row* and *column*.
Tells the current cursor position.
The cursor position is returned in RESULT.
It consists of two numbers, row and column.
Requires pre-registering, discussed under RXFUNCADD in
this book.
Example:

```
CALL SYSCURPOS 5, 10
SAY 'CURSOR WAS CURRENTLY AT' RESULT
PARSE VAR RESULT ROW COLUMN
SAY 'CURSOR IS AT ROW' ROW 'COLUMN' COLUMN
```

SYSCURSTATE Function (OS/2 Only)

CALL SYSCURSTATE *on or off*
Will not work under the Presentation Manager.
Displays or hides the cursor depending on *on or off*.
ON displays the cursor.
OFF hides the cursor.
Requires pre-registering, discussed under RXFUNCADD in
this book.
Example:

```
CALL SYSCURSTATE OFF
```

SYSDEREGISTEROBJECTCLASS Function (OS/2 Only)

CALL SYSDEREGISTEROBJECTCLASS *classname*
SAY RESULT

Removes an object class definition.
The opposite of SYSREGISTEROBJECTCLASS.
If it was successful a 1 is placed in RESULT.
If it was not, a 0 is placed in RESULT.
Requires pre-registering, discussed under RXFUNCADD in this book.
Example:

```
CALL SYSDEREGISTEROBJECTCLASS 'OLDOBJECTCLASS'
IF RESULT = 1
THEN SAY 'SUCCESSFUL'
```

SYSDESTROYOBJECT Function

CALL SYSDESTROYOBJECT *objectname*
SAY RESULT

Destroys an existing Workplace Shell object.
If it was successful a 1 is placed in RESULT.
If it was not, a 0 is placed in RESULT.
Requires pre-registering, discussed under RXFUNCADD in this book.
Example:

```
CALL SYSDESTROYOBJECT  'MYOBJECT'
IF RESULT = 1
THEN SAY 'SUCCESSFUL'
```

YSDRIVEINFO Function (OS/2 Only)

SAY SYSDRIVEINFO(*drive*)
Gives information about the disk *drive* specified.
Four words are returned: the disk drive letter, the number of
bytes of free space, the total capacity of the drive, and the
disk label.
Requires pre-registering, discussed under RXFUNCADD in
this book.
Example:

```
SAY SYSDRIVEINFO('C:')
     /* may return C: 12345678 83687424 MYDRIVE */
Parse Value Sysdriveinfo("C:") With Drive
   Free_space,
      Capacity Disk_label
```

YSDRIVEMAP Function (OS/2 Only)

SAY SYSDRIVEMAP()
Starting with the C: drive, gives the letters of the disk drives
that are accessible or in use.
Requires pre-registering, discussed under RXFUNCADD in
this book.
Example:

```
SAY SYSDRIVEMAP()    /* may return  C:  D:   */
```

SAY SYSDRIVEMAP(*drive*)
Starting with *drive*, gives the
letters of the disk drives that are accessible or in use.
Requires pre-registering, discussed under RXFUNCADD in
this book.
Example:

```
SAY SYSDRIVEMAP("D:")      /* may return  D:  E: */
```

SAY SYSDRIVEMAP(*drive,drive status*)
Starting with *drive*, gives the letters of the disk drives that are accessible or in use.
Requires pre-registering, discussed under RXFUNCADD in this book.

Drive status may be one of the following:

USED	the default
	all drives that are accessible, or in use
FREE	drives that are free or not in use
LOCAL	drives that are on your PC (workstation)
REMOTE	remote drives such as redirected LAN resources
DETACHED	drives that are detached LAN resources, for example a LAN drive assigned to you workstation but detached after a timeout

Example:
```
SAY SYSDRIVEMAP("C:","LOCAL")/* may return  C: D: *
```

SYSDROPFUNCS Function (OS/2 Only)

CALL SYSDROPFUNCS
Drops all the special functions that require pre-registering, making them unavailable until once again pre-registered.
Requires pre-registering, discussed under RXFUNCADD in this book.
Example:

```
CALL SYSDROPFUNCS
```

YSDSN TSO Only.

SAY SYSDSN(*dataset name*)

Tells if *dataset name* exists, or what its status is.

Returns:

OK   dataset name exists as specified.
MEMBER SPECIFIED BUT DATASET NOT PDS
MEMBER NOT FOUND
DATASET NOT FOUND
ERROR PROCESSING REQUESTED DATASET
PROTECTED DATASET
VOLUME NOT ON SYSTEM
UNAVAILABLE DATASET
INVALID DATASET NAME
MISSING DATASET NAME

Examples:

```
IF SYSDSN("JCL.CNTL(JOB001)") = "OK"
THEN
    DO
     "SUBMIT JCL.CNTL(JOB001)"
    END
ELSE
    DO
     SAY SYSDSN("JCL.CNTL(JOB001)")
    END
```

SYSFILEDELETE Function (OS/2 Only)

CALL SYSFILEDELETE '*file name*'
SAY RESULT

Deletes the file specified with file name.
Does not display an error message if the file doesn't exist.
It does, however, return a code number in RESULT that tells
you what happened.
Requires pre-registering, discussed under RXFUNCADD in
this book.

Codes returned in RESULT:

1	successful
2	file not found
3	path not found
5	access denied
26	not a DOS disk
32	sharing violation
36	sharing buffer exceeded
87	invalid parameter
206	file name exceeds range error

Example:

```
CALL SYSFILEDELETE 'TEMP.DAT'
IF RESULT = 0
THEN SAY 'DELETE SUCCESSFUL'
```

YSFILETREE Function (OS/2 Only)

CALL SYSFILETREE '*file specification*', '*REXX variable stem*'
Finds all files that match a *file specification*.
The file information is returned in REXX variables built upon
REXX variable stem.
If the stem specified is LINE., then information on the first file
found is returned in LINE.1.
The number of items returned is placed in the '0' element
based on the stem, LINE.0 in this case.
Requires pre-registering, discussed under RXFUNCADD in
this book.
Example:

```
CALL SYSFILETREE '*.CMD', 'LINE.'
SAY 'THE FILES THAT MATCH ARE:'
DO I = 1 TO LINE.0
  SAY LINE.I
END
```

YSFILESEARCH Function (OS/2 Only)

CALL SYSFILESEARCH '*string*', '*file*', '*REXX variable stem*', 'N'
Finds all lines in *file* that contain *string*.
The lines and their line numbers ('N' requests line numbers)
are returned in REXX variables built upon *REXX variable stem.*
If the stem specified is LINE., then the first line found is
returned in LINE.1.
The number of items returned is placed in the '0' element
based upon the stem, LINE.0 in this case.
Requires pre-registering, discussed under RXFUNCADD in
this book.
Example:

```
CALL SYSFILESEARCH 'IF','MYPROG.CMD','LINE.','N'
SAY 'THE LINES THAT CONTAIN IF ARE:'
DO I = 1 TO LINE.0
  SAY LINE.I
  /* how to separate line numbers from the line contents*/
  PARSE VAR LINE.I NUMBER CONTENTS
  SAY 'LINE NUMBER IS' NUMBER; SAY 'CONTENTS ARE' CONTENTS
END
```

SYSGETEA Function (OS/2 Only)

CALL SYSGETEA *'file', 'extended attribute', 'REXX variable*
IF RESULT = 0 THEN SAY *REXX variable*

Gives details on the *extended attribute* of *file* in *REXX variable*.
Note that *REXX variable* is in quotation marks or apostrophes.
Requires pre-registering, discussed under RXFUNCADD in
this book.

extended attributes of the workplace shell:

.CLASSINFO　　　　.ICON　　　　.LONGNAME　　　　.TYPE

Example:
```
File_name = "C:\testing\sample\abcdef.exe"

CALL SYSGETEA File_name, '.type','Filetype'
IF RESULT = 0 THEN SAY "The file type is " Filetype

CALL SYSGETEA File_name, '.longname','Longname'
IF RESULT = 0 THEN SAY "The long file name is "Longname

CALL SYSGETEA File_name, '.icon','Icon_name'
IF RESULT = 0 THEN SAY "The icon for this file is "Icon_name

CALL SYSGETEA File_name, '.classinfo','Class_info'
IF RESULT = 0 THEN SAY "The class of this file is "Class_info
```

SYSGETKEY Function (OS/2 Only)

CALL SYSGETKEY 'ECHO' or 'NOECHO'
SAY RESULT

Gets the next key pressed from the keyboard buffer.
The key pressed is returned in RESULT.
If the keyboard buffer is empty, it waits until a key is pressed.
The ENTER key does not have to be pressed.
Requires pre-registering, discussed under RXFUNCADD in this book.
Does not work properly under the Presentation Manager.

Example:
```
CALL SYSGETKEY 'ECHO'
SAY RESULT 'WAS KEY PRESSED'
```

Example that will show you the numeric equivalents for each key that you press.
Run this program and press each key on the keyboard and note what is displayed.
Notice that some keys, such as DELETE, give you two numbers.

```
/* REXX mykey.CMD */
Call Rxfuncadd "Sysgetkey", "rexxutil", "Sysgetkey"
Do 100
    Say "please press a key"
    Call Sysgetkey "ECHO"
    Say "You pressed" result "key. numeric equiv. is "
    C2X(Result)
End
```

SYSGETMESSAGE Function (OS/2 Only)

CALL SYSGETMESSAGE 'number'
SAY RESULT

Gets the text of the OS/2 message corresponding to *number*.
Requires pre-registering, discussed under RXFUNCADD in
this book.
Example:

```
CALL SYSGETMESSAGE '1'
SAY RESULT
```

SYSMKDIR Function (OS/2 Only)

CALL SYSMKDIR 'directory'
SAY RESULT

Creates a directory named *directory*.
No message is displayed in case of error.
Returns a code number in RESULT that tells if it was successful.
Requires pre-registering, discussed under RXFUNCADD in
this book.

Example:
```
CALL SYSMKDIR 'C:\REXXPRGS'
SAY RESULT
```

Codes returned in RESULT:

0	successful
2	file not found
3	path not found
5	access denied
26	not a DOS disk
87	invalid parameter
108	drive locked
206	file name exceeds range error

SYSOS2VER Function (OS/2 Only)

SAY SYSOS2VER()
Tells the current version of OS/2 you are running.
Requires pre-registering, discussed under RXFUNCADD in
this book.
Example:

```
SAY SYSOS2VER()
```

SYSPUTEA Function (OS/2 Only)

CALL SYSPUTEA *'file'*, *'extended attribute'*, *'value'*
SAY RESULT

Writes the *value* of *extended attribute* to *file*.
RESULT contains a 0 if the action was successful, otherwise it
contains an error code.
Requires pre-registering, discussed under RXFUNCADD in
this book.
Example:

```
CALL SYSPUTEA 'ABC.DAT', 'SECURITY','Unclassified'
IF RESULT = 0
THEN SAY 'SUCCESSFUL'
```

SYSQUERYCLASSLIST Function (OS/2 Only)

CALL SYSQUERYCLASSLIST *'REXX variable stem'*
Gives a complete list of registered object classes.
The classes are returned in REXX variables built upon
REXX variable stem).
If the stem specified is LINE., then the first class found is
returned in LINE.1.
The number of items returned is placed in the '0' element
based on the stem, LINE.0 in this case.
Requires pre-registering, discussed under RXFUNCADD in
this book.
Example:

```
CALL SYSQUERYCLASSLIST 'LINE.'
SAY 'THE CLASSES REGISTERED ARE:'
DO I = 1 TO LINE.0
  SAY LINE.I
END
```

SYSREGISTEROBJECTCLASS Function (OS/2 Only)

CALL SYSREGISTEROBJECTCLASS *'class name'*, *'module name'*
SAY RESULT

Registers a new object class definition, using *class name* as a
name and *module name* as the module containing the object
definition.
RESULT contains a 1 if the action was successful, otherwise it
contains a 0.
Requires pre-registering, discussed under RXFUNCADD in
this book.
Example:

```
CALL SYSREGISTEROBJECTCLASS ,'NEWOBJECT', 'NEWDLL'
IF RESULT = 1
THEN SAY 'SUCCESSFUL'
```

SYSRMDIR Function (OS/2 Only)

CALL SYSRMDIR '*directory*'
SAY RESULT

Deletes a directory named *directory*.
Does not display an error message in case of failure.
Returns a code number in RESULT that tells if it
was successful.
Requires pre-registering, discussed under RXFUNCADD in
this book.
Example:

```
CALL SYSRMDIR 'REXXPRGS'
SAY RESULT
```

Codes returned in RESULT:

0	successful
2	file not found
3	path not found
5	access denied
16	current directory
26	not a DOS disk
87	invalid parameter
108	drive locked
206	file name exceeds range error

SYSSEARCHPATH Function (OS/2 Only)

CALL SYSSEARCHPATH *environment variable, file name*
SAY RESULT

Searches a path specified in *environment variable* looking
for a *file*.
Environment variables are set in OS/2 in CONFIG.SYS, or in
a SET OS/2 command.
The normal environment variables to use here are PATH
and DPATH.
Returns the full file specification in RESULT, if successful,
otherwise returns a null string.
Requires pre-registering, discussed under RXFUNCADD in
this book.
Example:

```
CALL SYSSEARCHPATH 'PATH', 'MYPROG01.CMD'
IF RESULT = ""
THEN SAY 'COULD NOT FIND FILE'
ELSE SAY RESULT "is the full file specification"
```

SYSSETICON Function (OS/2 Only)

CALL SYSSETICON *file name, icon file name*
SAY RESULT

Associates an icon found in *icon file name* with a file named
file name.
Returns a 1 if successful, a 0 if not.
Requires pre-registering, discussed under RXFUNCADD in
this book.
Example:

```
CALL SYSSETICON 'ABC.DAT', 'ABC.ICO'
IF RESULT = 1
THEN SAY 'SUCCESSFUL'
ELSE  SAY 'COULD NOT ASSOCIATE '
```

SYSSLEEP Function (OS/2 Only)

CALL SYSSLEEP *seconds*
Puts the program into a suspended state for the specified number of seconds.
You may interrupt the program with CTRL and C or CTRL and Break.
Requires pre-registering, discussed under RXFUNCADD in this book.
Example:

```
CALL SYSSLEEP 1        /* zzzzzzzz */
```

SYSTEMPFILENAME Function (OS/2 Only)

FILE_NAME = SYSTEMPFILENAME('*partial file specification*')
SAY FILE_NAME

Gives a file name that does not currently exist and that can be safely used as a temporary file name.
Partial file specification consists of a drive, a directory, and a file name containing one or more question marks (?).
This function replaces the question marks with numbers that it chooses.
Requires pre-registering, discussed under RXFUNCADD in this book.
Example:

```
TEMP_FILE =  SYSTEMPFILENAME('C:\REXXPRGS\TEMPFILE.???')
RESULT = TEMP_FILE
IF TEMP_FILE ="" THEN SAY 'COULD NOT PRODUCE TEMP NAME'
ELSE SAY TEMP_FILE 'IS THE TEMP FILE NAME'
  /*will give something like C:\REXXPRGS\TEMPFILE.123*/
```

SYSTEXTSCREENREAD Function (OS/2 Only)

SCREEN_CH = SYSTEXTSCREENREAD(*row, column, length*)
SAY 'READ THESE CHARACTERS' SCREEN_CH

Reads characters off the screen.
Starts reading at *row* and *column*, and reads *length* characters.
Will not work under the Presentation Manager.
Requires pre-registering, discussed under RXFUNCADD in this book.
Example:

```
SCREEN_CH = SYSTEXTSCREENREAD(10, 20, 40)
SAY 'READ THESE CHARACTERS' SCREEN_CH
```

SYSTEXTSCREENSIZE Function (OS/2 Only)

SCREEN_SIZE = SYSTEXTSCREENSIZE()
SAY 'SCREEN SIZE IS' SCREEN_SIZE

Tells the screen size with two numbers: rows and columns.
Will not work under the Presentation Manager.
Requires pre-registering, discussed under RXFUNCADD in this book.
Example:

```
SCREEN_SIZE = SYSTEXTSCREENSIZE()
SAY 'SCREEN SIZE IS' SCREEN_SIZE
PARSE VAR SCREENSIZE ROWS COLUMNS
SAY ROWS 'ROWS'
SAY COLUMNS 'COLUMNS'
```

SYSVAR Function (TSO Only)

SAY SYSVAR(*type of info desired*)
Retrieves information about one system variable at a time.

type of info desired:

SYSPREF	the prefix that TSO is putting in front of dataset names without apostrophes.
SYSPROC	the logon procedure used to log on
SYSUID	the userid you logged on with
SYSLTERM	number of lines available on the terminal screen
SYSWTERM	width of the terminal screen
SYSENV	environment you are executing in
	FORE in normal foreground TSO
	BACK when executed thru JCL
SYSICMD	the name by which the program was executed implicitly
SYSISPF	ACTIVE if dialogue manager is available
	NOT ACTIVE if not
SYSNEST	YES if program executed from another program/CLIST
	NO if executed directly from TSO
SYSPCMD	the most recently executed TSO command
SYSSCMD	the most recently executed TSO subcommand
SYSCPU	how many CPU seconds used so far
SYSHSM	a null if HSM not available, or a number indicating release of HSM available
SYSLRACF	a null if RACF is not installed, or a number indicating level of RACF available
SYSRACF	AVAILABLE if RACF available
	NOT AVAILABLE if RACF not available
	NOT INSTALLED if RACF not installed
SYSSRV	how many SRM service units used so far
SYSTSOE	level of TSO/E installed

Syntax error if wrong type is specified.
Examples:

```
SAY SYSVAR("SYSENV")    /* FORE */
SAY SYSVAR("SYSUID")    /* TSOU01 (or other TSO userid) */
```

SYSWAITNAMEDPIPE Function (OS/2 Only)

CALL SYSWAITNAMEDPIPE "*pipe*"
SAY RESULT

Waits for a named *pipe*.
The success or failure is reported in RESULT.
A 0 indicates that the action is complete, a 2 that the pipe
could not be found, and 231 that there was a timeout.
Requires pre-registering, discussed under RXFUNCADD in
this book.
Example:

```
CALL SYSWAITNAMEDPIPE '\PIPE\nameofpipe'
SAY RESULT
```

TE TSO and CMS Command (TSO and CMS Only)
Turns off interactive debug.

 • On TSO, it may be executed after an attention interrupt
obtained by pressing the PA1 key or the ATTN key.

 • On CMS, it may be executed as a CMS immediate command
when the screen is displaying MORE . . . in the lower right.

TIME Function

SAY TIME()   Returns the time of day formatted as 14:22:55.

SAY TIME(*type*)   Returns the time of day formatted according to *type*

Types:
(omitted)	14:22:55
C	"Civil time" 10:26pm
H	Hours since midnight: 14
L	"Long" includes microseconds
M	Minutes since midnight: 22
S	Seconds since midnight: 55
E (first time)	Starts elapsed time counter
E (second time)	Gives elapsed time in seconds, since first E
R	Resets elapsed time counter to zero

Example:

```
SAY TIME('H')                  /* 14 (or other hour) */
```

TRACE Function

CALL TRACE 'trace option'
Changes the trace option to the one specified. Same as using the command TRACE *trace option*.
Trace options:

N	Normal, the default: trace Syntax errors
E	Error: trace environment commands that don't work properly
F	Failure: trace environment commands that abend or don't exist
C	Commands: under OS/2 this is on by default in OS/2 Window/Full Screen turn off by placing "@" before the command, as in "@DIR" under OS/2 this is off by default in presentation manager window turn it on by TRACE C
R	Results: display results of REXX verbs
I	Intermediate: display intermediate results of REXX verbs
L	Labels: display labels that are entered
S	Scan: do not execute anything; just do a partial check for syntax
O	Off: turn off tracing

SAY TRACE()
Returns the current trace setting

Example:

```
CALL TRACE I
SAY TRACE()              /* I */
```

TRACE Instruction
Controls tracing and interactive debugging.
Examples (starting with those that trace the least and ending with those that trace the most):

TRACE !	Nothing traced, **don't execute TSO or CMS commands.** non-functional under OS/2
TRACE !C (Commands)	Trace TSO or CMS commands; **don't execute TSO or CMS commands.** non-functional under OS/2
TRACE !R (Results)	Trace labels, commands, REXX verbs, changed variables; **don't execute TSO or CMS commands.** non-functional under OS/2
TRACE !I (Intermediate)	Trace labels, commands, REXX verbs, changed variables, Intermediate results ex: C = (4*3) + 2; **don't execute TSO or CMS commands.** non-functional under OS/2
TRACE O (Off)	Nothing traced.
TRACE N (Normal)	Trace Environment commands that (the default) fail/error out; REXX verbs that fail.

TRACE F (Failure)

Trace Environment commands that terminate abnormally, or don't exist.

TRACE E (Error)

Trace Environment commands that don't work.

TRACE C (Commands)

Trace Environment commands. under OS/2 this is on by default in OS/2 Window/Full Screen turn off by placing "@" before the command, as in "@DIR" under OS/2 this is off by default in presentation manager window turn it on by TRACE C

TRACE L (Labels)

Trace labels.

TRACE A (All)

Trace labels, commands, REXX verbs.

TRACE S (Scan)

Trace labels, commands, and REXX verbs but don't execute *anything.*

TRACE R (Results)

Trace labels, commands, REXX verbs, changed variables.

TRACE I (Intermediate)

Trace labels, commands, REXX verbs, changed variables; intermediate results ex: C = (4*3) + 2.

TRACE ?R (Results)

Trace labels, commands, REXX verbs, changed variables; **interactive debug**.

TRACE ?I (Intermediate)

Trace labels, commands, REXX verbs, changed variables, intermediate results ex: C = (4*3) + 2; **interactive debug**.

TS TSO and CMS Command (TSO and CMS Only)
Turns on interactive debug with an automatic TRACE RESULTS.

- On TSO, it may be executed after an attention interrupt obtained by pressing the PA1 key or the ATTN key.

- On CMS, it may be executed as a CMS immediate command when the screen is displaying MORE . . . in the lower right. Turning on interactive debug outside of the program with an operating system command
CMS   SET EXECTRAC ON
TSO   EXECUTIL TS
OS/2   SET RXTRACE=ON

TRANSLATE Function

NEW_STRING = TRANSLATE
(*string, output table, input table*)
Translates *string*, converting any occurrence of character 1 in *input table* to character 1 of *output table*; character 2 to character 2,and so on.
Examples:

```
/* note there is 1 space after NOYEM*/
SAY TRANSLATE('DINERO','NOYEM ','NIREDO')   /* MONEY */

SAY TRANSLATE('HI','abcdefghij','ABCDEFGHIJ')/* hi */
```

NEW_STRING = TRANSLATE(*string, output table, input table, pad*)
Translates *string*, converting any occurrence of character 1 in *input table* to character 1 of *output table*; character 2 to character 2,and so on.
Pad character is used if there is a character in the input table, but not in the output table.

Examples:

```
SAY TRANSLATE('HI','abcdefgh','ABCDEFGHIJ','!')/* h! */
```

NEW_STRING = TRANSLATE(*string*)
Converts *string* to upper case.
Example:

```
SAY TRANSLATE('abcdefghi')          /* ABCDEFGHI */
```

TRUNC Function

SAY TRUNC(*number, decimal places*)
Returns the *number* with *decimal places* decimal places.
Truncates or zero fills as needed.
Examples:

```
SAY TRUNC(1234.5,4)   /* 1234.5000 */
SAY TRUNC(1234.5,0)   /* 1234  */
```

USERID Function (TSO and CMS Only)

SAY USERID()
Returns the userid you are logged on with.
Example:

```
SAY USERID()     /* possibly TSOU01 or VMUSR1 */
```

VALUE Function

SAY VALUE(*symbol*)
Returns the contents of *symbol* after resolving it as a variable.
Examples:

```
PROG_NAME  = 'COBOL'
COBOL = 'ENGLISH-LIKE'
SAY VALUE('PROG_NAME')                 /* COBOL */
SAY VALUE(PROG_NAME)               /* ENGLISH-LIKE */
```

VERIFY Function

SAY VERIFY(*string1, string2*)
Are all the characters of *string1* made up of characters found in *string2*?
Returns a 0 if yes, otherwise the position of first character in *string1* that is not in *string2*.
Examples:

```
SAY VERIFY('SUSAN','ABNTUSV') /* 0 */
SAY VERIFY('SUSAN','ABCDEFG') /* 1 */
```

WORD Function

SAY WORD(*string, n*)
Returns the *n*'th word in *string*.
Example:

```
SAY WORD('ET PHONE HOME COLLECT',2)     /* PHONE */
```

WORDINDEX Function

SAY WORDINDEX(*string, n*)
Returns the character position of the *n*'th word in *string*.
Example:

```
SAY WORDINDEX('ET PHONE HOME COLLECT',2)/* 4 */
```

WORDLENGTH Function

SAY WORDLENGTH(*string, n*)
Returns the length of the *n*'th word in *string*.
Example:

```
SAY WORDLENGTH('ET PHONE HOME COLLECT',2)/* 5 */
```

WORDPOS Function

SAY WORDPOS(*phrase, string*)

Searches for *phrase* in *string*.
Counts the words in *string* until there is a match.
Returns the word count.
Example:

```
SAY WORDPOS('PHONE HOME','ET PHONE HOME COLLECT') /* 2 */
```

SAY WORDPOS(*phrase, string, starting word*)

Searches for *phrase* in *string*, starting with *starting word*.
Counts the words in *string* until there is a match.
Returns the word count.
Example:

```
SAY WORDPOS('HI','HI HO HI HO OFF TO WORK WE GO',2) /* 3 */
```

WORDS Function

SAY WORDS(*string*)

Counts the words in *string*. Returns the word count.
Example:

```
SAY WORDS('ET PHONE HOME COLLECT') /* 4 */
```

XRANGE Function

SAY XRANGE(*starting character, ending character*)
You specify a starting character and an ending character. The function returns all the characters that lie between the two. Example:

```
SAY XRANGE('A','D')            /* ABCD */
```

Unprintable and nondisplay characters may be specified as Hexadecimal constants.
Examples:

```
SAY XRANGE('F1'X,'F5'X)        /* 12345 */

SAY XRANGE('00'X,'09'X)        /* 00010203040506070809
   (This is the Hex value of what returned but is unprintable.
   The following example will clarify.)*/
IF XRANGE('00'X,'09'X) = '00010203040506070809'X
THEN SAY 'IT IS EQUAL' /* true */
Also, note this:
SAY C2X(XRANGE('00'X,'09'X))   /* 00010203040506070809 */
```

X2B Function

SAY X2B(*hexstring*)
Converts *hexstring* to binary but displayed in character format.
Example:

```
SAY X2B('F0')           /* 11110000 */
```

X2C Function

SAY X2C(*hexstring*)
Converts *hexstring* to character.
Example:

```
SAY X2C('313233')            /* 123 */
/* Note: same as SAY '313233'X */
```

X2D Function

SAY X2D(*hexstring*)
Converts *hexstring* to decimal.
Examples:

```
SAY X2D(81)                  /* 129 */
SAY X2D('F')                 /* 15 */
SAY X2D('F1F2F3')            /* 15856371 */
SAY X2D(313233)              /* 3224115 */
```

Index